THE SPIRIT OF JUDAISM.

THE

SPIRIT OF JUDAISM.

BY

JOSEPHINE LAZARUS.

Essay Index Reprint Series

 BOOKS FOR LIBRARIES PRESS
FREEPORT, NEW YORK

First Published 1895
Reprinted 1972

Library of Congress Cataloging in Publication Data

Lazarus, Josephine, 1846-1910.
 The spirit of Judaism.

 (Essay index reprint series)
 Reprint of the 1895 ed.
 1. Judaism--Addresses, essays, lectures. I. Title.
BM45.L34 1972   296   77-38031
ISBN 0-8369-2602-1

PRINTED IN THE UNITED STATES OF AMERICA
BY
NEW WORLD BOOK MANUFACTURING CO., INC.
HALLANDALE, FLORIDA 33009

CONTENTS.

———◆———

	PAGE
THE JEWISH QUESTION	7
THE OUTLOOK OF JUDAISM	28
JUDAISM, OLD AND NEW	70
THE CLAIM OF JUDAISM	101
THE TASK OF JUDAISM	133
EPILOGUE	192

THE SPIRIT OF JUDAISM.

THE JEWISH QUESTION.

TO approach the Jewish question is
to be confronted with every great
question of the day, — social, political,
financial, humanitarian, national, and
religious. Each phase should be treated
by an expert and specialist, for in each
lies a deep, urgent, practical problem
which requires the wisest and most skilled
handling; but, however discussed or dealt
with, there is one point of view which
should never be lost sight of, — namely,
the point of view of humanity. All other

standpoints must be merged or held in abeyance. First and foremost, we must be human if we would raise our voice on so human a theme, involving the lives and destinies of so many unhappy human beings.

It is a sorry spectacle that the world presents at the end of our emancipated nineteenth century, — hundreds and thousands of our fellow-creatures, men, women, and innocent children, driven from their homes, helpless, destitute, and distracted, flying where? whither? No one knows, for in turn each nation threatens to shut them out as outcasts and pariahs.

Who, then, are these alien wretches, with speech unlike our own, with ways and customs peculiar to themselves; and what is their crime? we ask. There are those who will tell us that they are usurers, eating the flesh and grinding the faces of the poor; others will say that

they are traitors, plotting against their
sovereign rulers; others will call them
enemies of the Christ; and again others
will lay at their door nameless cruel
charges of ignorant fanaticism. Their
crime is legion, and yet one word sums
it up, — they are Jews. "Hep! Hep!"
It is an old battle-cry, old as Christendom,
but it rings to-day fresh from the nations.
Russia leads with brute violence, sweeping them from the soil; Germany follows with lofty phrases, pulpit and paper
warfare; even liberal France takes the
alarm; and occasionally a small British
voice pipes in the chorus, "Christians,
beware! The Jew is richer, is sharper
than you. Look to your interest and
your purse. Royalty is at his feet, the
stock exchange belongs to him, and the
press is his organ."

But in justice to humanity let us
hasten to add that there is another side.

In all the countries we have named, Russia perhaps alone excepted, all earnest and right-minded Christians, no less than Jews, are aghast at the sinister revelations, and are doing what they can to stem the current and to enter their protest against so barbarous a reaction. But this new outbreak of hatred and antagonism, after centuries of progress and enlightenment, is a phenomenon so startling that it calls for examination more searching, and deeper comprehension, than it generally receives.

Whether the tragic history of the Jews redounds more to their glory and martyrdom than to the honour of the Christians, is not the point which will throw any special light upon the subject just now; but both Jews and Christians alike — whoever studies with impartiality the annals of the past — must be struck with the ever-recurring features, the mask, of

this ugly monster of persecution, grown
so familiar through the ages. History
seems to move backward or in a circle;
here are the same grievances as in the
days of the Cæsars, the same jealous mis-
trust and animosity, the same cruel and
exaggerated retribution. The classic
writers of pagan antiquity are full of
the most scornful and contemptuous
references. A fair-minded writer of to-
day [1] says of the Jew : —

"Even his virtues are of the unsym-
pathetic sort. Temperate, uniformly
chaste and industrious, a faithful hus-
band and marvellously good father, a
peaceful and law-abiding citizen in whatever country he may be, yet no one
wants him as a settler; and the mis-
eries of the Russian Jew had to mount
up in the scale until they suggested the

[1] Harold Frederic, in the " Times " of October 12,
1891.

horrors of the Spanish Inquisition before the world really took much interest."

To seek for the origin and explanation of so radical an incompatibility would be wellnigh a hopeless task; but much more useful and important would be to draw what lesson we could for the future, which would help toward the solution, however distant, of so complicated and grievous a problem.

Of all the schemes of colonisation, the one that appeals most to the imagination is the return to Palestine. On the spot where they once were a great nation, and amid surroundings that seem better suited to their traditions and highest destiny than our Western conditions, they might again put forth some great spiritual idea, some new blossoming of the genius which is surely theirs. But the object of the present study is not to offer any suggestion or panacea, but rather, if possible,

to lift the subject upon a broader plane;
to rise for the moment above the human
drama of strife and suffering which is
being enacted, into the region of pure
ideas and principles, — for it is here
that the warfare of Israel is truly accomplished, — and to discover, if we may,
the spiritual facts and forces that are at
play, the ultimate result to which they
point, and the working of divine and
eternal truth through so much human
error and sacrifice.

And in endeavouring to do this, it is
to the Jews rather than to the Christians
that we would address ourselves, — to
the advanced and liberated Jews of
Europe and America; for it is with them
that a great responsibility rests, and a
great opportunity. Thoroughly aroused
to the material exigencies of the situation, collectively and individually giving
their best energies, spending their money

like water, the reproach can never be
brought against the Jew that he has
failed to respond to the cry of his brother
in distress, or that prosperity has made
him forget the endless adversity of his
race. But in providing a home for his
hapless comrade, in crowding him into
the overcrowded ranks of the toiling
masses, and initiating him into the fierce
struggle of modern selfishness, has he
done all his duty? Or even in holding
out the hand of religious fellowship, and
helping him to the full and free exercise
of the immemorial customs and traditions of his race, is the free, untram-
melled Israelite doing the best and the
highest that his advantages and opportunities can suggest for this belated new-
comer, who emerges, as it were, out of
the Middle Ages into the bright light of
a new day, and the broad rushing stream
of Western ideas ? And in order to

answer these questions, we must endeavour, if possible, clearly to understand the true status of the Jew in modern civilisation : the moral and material conditions under which he is allowed to advance; the ideals and aims which he sets for himself, — in other words, the true import and content of modern Judaism under its most favourable circumstances and environment.

Broadly speaking, we come upon three classes of Jews in the community, sometimes sharply defined, and again merging into one another.

First, there is the remnant of orthodox Jews, mostly of Spanish and Portuguese descent, but with greatly enlarged contingent now of Russian and Polish immigration, who cling without shadow of turning to the primeval faith, strictly observing the rigid form of the Sabbath, the whole dietary régime, every text of the law, every feast and every fast that commemorates a religious or a national event. If we go into the most modern of their synagogues we shall find it exactly as in the ancient days, — the entrance always facing the east ; the reader's desk in the middle, with its tall candlesticks ; the perpetual lamp burning before the tabernacle where the scrolls of the law are contained, wrapped in their silken mantles and overtopped with their silvery tinkling bells; the men and women seated apart, — the women in their upper gallery, the men with covered head, and over their shoulders the white and blue-bordered silken scarfs, with fringes knotted according to custom to represent the Hebrew characters of the law ; the service entirely in Hebrew, chanted by the reader with response by the congregation, and occasionally a chorus of male voices. No need to question these venerable believers. Their faith is as old as Moses, and their code, the one he formulated four thousand years ago, elaborated into a system more complete than anything that has ever been devised, a subtle interweaving of precept and practice so that every action of the life is regulated according to some Levitical command, and every command is externalised into some outward fact and observance. In the eyes of such conformists Judaism is a sacred trust, at once national, religious, and ancestral, to be handed down intact from generation to generation; and the Jews are a special, consecrated race, favoured and chosen of God to be the bearers of his Word unto men.

Breaking away from this extreme formalism, with its excessive and difficult minutiæ, we find the second class, — the reform Jews, who constitute an always increasing body, being constantly re-

cruited from the orthodox ranks. Still
following the traditions, observing the
seventh day as the Sabbath, the solemn
fast, and all the great holidays, they have
generally emancipated themselves from
much of the ceremonial law, especially
the dietary restrictions, and the whole
code and practice of life have more scope
and freedom. In the synagogue — or
temple, as they prefer to call it — the
service is still for the most part in
Hebrew ; but there is an organ and choir,
and men and women sit together, the
men with uncovered heads. Here again
the principles are not difficult to define,
although somewhat less stable and consistent, and opening the way to the third
class, which reveals elements more complex and anomalous, and horizons in-
finitely larger but more vague.

And in regard to this third class we
cannot do better than freely quote from the

pages of the " Revue des Deux Mondes "[1] by Leroy Beaulieu, whose masterly and comprehensive survey of the whole subject has nowhere been equalled. Rejecting, he says, as effete and outworn, the legal and ritualistic tradition, the Jews of this class fasten upon the race tradition, the Messianic hope, and belief in the destiny of Israel again to give a religion to the world, " but this time a religion without inconvenient customs or unreasonable dogma, without miracles or any mysteries." In this case, however, so radical and complete is the separation from their orthodox co-religionists that the very corner-stone of the one becomes the stumbling-block in the eyes of the others, the obstacle which in all ages has prevented Judaism from arriving at its legitimate and universal supremacy. " Break your chains," say

[1] For February 15, May 1, and July 15, 1891.

these disciples of progress. " Proclaim the Unity of God, the sanctity of the moral law ; and you have a faith at once human and divine, both large and simple enough to satisfy all mankind."

A beautiful dream, says Leroy Beaulieu, and entirely characteristic of the race. But will it truly satisfy any one, — above all, their brethren the Jews themselves, who look upon their very existence as conditioned upon precisely the things they are asked to give up ? Without rites, without dogma and formal cult, can they have a religion at all ? he asks ; can they have Judaism, at all events ? What remains when all outward form and semblance has departed from that which was built and buttressed upon outward form ? What substance, what essence, is left of the Judaic idea, save an abstract and far-away deism, or a humanitarianism more delusive still, leading down the banal sliding-scale of unbelief ?

Such a question is fully justified when we see foremost among the ranks of agnosticism, scepticism, and materialism so large a preponderance of Jews that this too is brought in reproach against them. For there is no more noteworthy and singular fact in the whole history of this singular people than the constant and uniform recurrence of the two opposite types, — the extremes of idealism and materialism, — which the race presents. While their whole existence and survival are based upon a spiritual idea, there is no people whose kingdom is so absolutely of this world, and who are so prone, so apt, so eager, to take advantage of all its opportunities.

In the face of all these contradictions, where, then, shall we find the rallying-point, where the real unity, the central sun which shall illumine not Judaism alone, but all mankind ? Not for an

instant do we doubt that each of the
sects we have described has vitality
enough to survive for long years to come ;
but it can survive only as a sect, with
all the limitations and disabilities that
the name involves. And the world is
breaking free from these narrow lines.
Everywhere there are signs of a spiritual
awakening and expansion which every
religion must meet and fulfil, or be found
wanting. Even science leads now to the
portals of " The Unknown God." Christianity is undergoing a profound modification, and a divine spark still lingers
in Judaism.

But in order to kindle this into a flame,
a deeper current is needed, a more glowing impulse, and that quickening breath
of the spirit which does not seem to
animate modern Jewish life and thought.
It is not enough to rehearse the glories
of the past, nor to point to names, dis-

tinguished though they be in the world
of to-day. The need of Israel in the
present and its true greatness in the past
consist in spiritual leadership. Above
the inert mass, the dull crowd of Pharisees and Scribes dwelling within the life-
less body of the Law, have arisen the
divinely gifted men, the prophets and
seers of the world, who saw God and
spoke face to face with him. From
Abraham to St. Paul they were men who
threw off the idolatries and superstitions
of the times, the bondage of the letter,
and proclaimed the inner, not the outer,
law, — the spirit, not the form. For they
knew the Presence ; " the burden of the
valley of vision " lay upon them.

And this is the lack with the Judaism
of our day, — the inward living voice, the
heaven-sent message. Loyal to the word,
to the faith and God of their fathers
Abraham, Isaac, and Jacob, they have

nailed the Law upon the door-posts, and bound it as a sign upon the brow and hands, and fringed their garments with it. More than this, they have kept the Commandments, and preserved themselves a pure and moral race. But even as a man may bestow all his goods to feed the poor, and give his body to be burned, and yet may not have charity, so a man may keep the Law and the Commandments and give his body to be burned, and yet not have religion.

"Who is blind but my servant; or deaf as my messenger that I sent? Who is blind as he that is perfect, and blind as the Lord's servant?

"Seeing many things, but thou observest not; opening the ears, but he heareth not."

For religion is not alone a doing, but a being, a quality of soul, a motive power and principle. It is the hidden force which

binds the seen to the unseen, the finite
to the infinite, the human to the divine;
which solves and fuses the whole nature
of man, lifting him beyond the bounda-
ries of time and space, the illusions of
matter and sense, into the realm of true
and imperishable being. To enter this
realm it is not necessary to pass away
from earth, but simply to be freed from
earthly considerations and limitations,
to rise above earthly prizes and rewards,
and to come into spiritual possession;
for this is the kingdom of heaven, although we may be still upon earth, we
may suffer, and even fall into sin. But,
dwelling in darkness and in the shadow
of death, we may yet see light and life.

Deep in the heart of Judaism is enshrined a sacred, an immortal word, —
duty, — which makes of man a moral
being, and links him to the moral source
of the universe. Deep in the heart of

Christianity is enshrined a sacred and immortal word, — love, — which makes of man a spiritual being, and links him to the divine source of all life. Humanity needs both these words in order to become the perfect creation it was meant to be. The one gives the conscience, the other the heart, of mankind ; the one is the masculine, the other the feminine, element of the world. Judaism gives the Ten Commandments, and Christianity the Beatitudes ; but only the two together can yield the perfect ideal, — the love that is simply the highest duty, and duty that is lost in love.

And in order to come into this closer, higher union, into the faith which makes humanity whole, and not a thing of parts, and the truth which makes men free, fixed and formal codes must disappear ; the outer framework of history and theology must fall away, and spirit be left free to seek Spirit. Then, and then only, will life have its whole meaning, as part of a larger life whose beginning and end are hidden from mortal vision. Religion will have its full sway, and yet there will be none who persecute and none who are persecuted; "for the earth shall be full of the knowledge of the Lord, as the waters cover the sea."

January, 1892.

THE OUTLOOK OF JUDAISM.

THE nineteenth century has had its surprises. The position of the Jew to-day is one of these, both for the Jew himself and for most enlightened Christians. There were certain facts we thought forever laid at rest, certain conditions and contingencies that could never confront us again, certain war-cries that could not be raised. In this last decade of our civilisation, however, we have been rudely awakened from our false dream of security — it may be to a higher calling and destiny than we had yet foreseen.

I do not wish to emphasise the painful facts by dwelling on them, or even pointing them out. We are all aware of them, and whenever Jews and Christians can come together on equal terms, ignoring difference and opposition and injury, it is well that they should do so. At the same time we must not shut our eyes, nor, like the ostrich, bury our head in the sand. The situation, which is so grave a one, must be bravely and honestly faced, the crisis met, the problem frankly stated in all its bearings, so that the whole truth may be brought to light, if possible. We are a little apt to look on one side only of the shield, especially when our sense of justice and humanity is stung, and the cry of the oppressed and persecuted — our brothers — rings in our ears.

As we all know, the effect of persecution is to strengthen solidarity. The Jew who never was a Jew before becomes one when the vital spot is touched, " the Jew " is thrust upon him, whether he would or not, and made an insult and reproach. When we are attacked as Jews we do not strike back angrily, but we coil up in our shell of Judaism and intrench ourselves more strongly than before.

Thrown back constantly upon itself, Judaism thus remains to a great extent a separate factor, an isolated and uncombined element in modern culture. The Jews themselves, both from natural habit and force of circumstance, have been accustomed to dwell along their own lines of thought and life, absorbed in their own point of view, almost to the exclusion of outside opinion. Indeed, it is this power of concentration in their own pursuits that insures their success in most things they set out to do. They have been content for the most part to guard the truth they hold, rather than spread it or even thoroughly weigh it in the scale along with other truth in the world. In spite of individual exceptions, of outward affiliation, and the identification of external interests and occupation, the Jews as a body have not generally made an integral part of the community in which they live. The life flows side by side, but does not mingle at its source; and they are forced to take refuge in their historic past and familiar race-traditions from an alien world which does not wholly accept or understand them, and where they are not quite at home.

At the same time, amid favourable surroundings and easy circumstance, many of us had ceased to take it very deeply or seriously that we were Jews. We had grown to look upon it merely as an accident of birth, for which we were not called upon to make any sacrifice, and which in our ordinary life and daily

transactions with our fellow-men we
tried to ignore, so as to make ourselves
as much as possible like our neighbours,
neither better nor worse than the people
around us. But with a painful shock we
are suddenly made aware of it as a det-
riment, and we shrink at once back
into ourselves, hurt in our most sensitive
point, our pride wounded to the quick,
our most sacred feelings, as we believe,
outraged and trampled upon.

But our very attitude proves that
something is wrong with us. Persecution does not touch us; we do not feel
it when we have an idea large enough
and close enough to our hearts to sus-
tain and console us. The martyrs of old
did not feel the fires of the stake, the
arrows that pierced their flesh. The
Jews of the olden time danced to their
death with praise and song and joyful
shouts of Hallelujah. They were will-

ing to die for that which was their life
and more than their life to them.

But the martyrdom of the present day
is a strange and novel one, almost a
sordid one, that has no grace or glory
about it, and of which we are not proud.
We have not chosen, and perhaps would
not choose it. Many of us scarcely
know the cause for which we suffer, and
therefore we feel every pang, every cut
of the lash. For our own sake, then,
and still more perhaps for those who
come after us and to whom we bequeath
our Judaism, it behooves us to find out
just what it means to us, and what it
holds for us to live by. In other words,
what is the content and significance of
modern Judaism in the world to-day,
not only for us personally as Jews, but
for the world at large? What power
has it as a spiritual influence? And as
such, what is its share or part in the

large life of humanity, in the broad current and movement of the time? What
actuality has it, and what possible un-
foldment in the future?

And as we shall very soon discover, it is
much easier to ask these questions than
to answer them. Indeed, no sooner have
we put them than we are at once confronted with every phase of sentiment,
every shade and variety of opinion. We
sweep the whole gamut of modern rest-
less thought, of shifting beliefs and unbelief, from the depths of superstition,
as well as of scepticism and materialism, to the cold heights of agnosticism;
from the most rigid and uncompromising
formalism, or a sincere piety, to a humanitarianism so broad that it has almost
eliminated God, or a deism so vast and
distant that it has almost eliminated
humanity.

Nothing is more curious than this

range and diversity of conviction from
a centre of unity; for the Jewish idea
survives through every contradiction,
as the race, the type, persists through
every modification of climate and lo-
cality, and every varying nationality.
Clear and distinct, we can trace it
through history; and as the present can
best be read by the light of the past,
I should like briefly to review the ideas
on which our existence is based and our
identity sustained.

What an endless perspective! Age
after age unrolls, nations appear and
disappear, and still we follow and find
them. Back to the very morning of
time, before the primal mists had lifted
from the world, while yet there were
giants in the earth, and the sons of God
mingled with the daughters of men, we
come upon their dim and mythical be-
ginnings, — a tribe of wanderers in

Eastern lands, roaming beside the water-
ways, feeding their flocks upon the hill-
sides, leading their camels across the
lonely desert wastes, and pitching their
tents beneath the high star-studded
skies; from the first a people much
alone with their own souls and Nature,
brought to face the Infinite, self-centred,
brooding, and conscious of a something,
they knew not what, — a Power not
themselves, — that led their steps and
walked and talked with men.

Already in those earliest days great
types loom up among them, — the patri-
archal leaders, large, tribal, composite
figures rather than actual persons, and
yet touched with human traits and personality, moving about in pastoral and
domestic scenes; men already, in their
own crude way, pre-occupied of God
and His dealings with themselves and
with the world.

Upon a background of myth, and yet in a sense how bold, how clear stands Moses, the man of God, who saw the world aflame with Deity, — the burning bush, the flaming mountain-top, the fiery cloud, — leading his people from captivity, and who heard pronounced the divine and everlasting name, the unpronounceable, the ineffable I Am!

In Moses, above all, whether we look upon him as semi-historic or a purely symbolic figure, the genius of the Hebrew race is typified, the fundamental note of Judaism is struck, — the Word that rings forever after through the ages, which is the Law spoken by God Himself, with trumpet sound, midst thunderings and lightning from heaven.

Whatever of true or false, of fact or legend, hangs about it, we have in the Mosaic conception the moral ideal of the Hebrews, a code divinely sanctioned and ordained, the absolute imperative of duty, a transcendent law laid upon man, which he must perforce obey in order that he may live. " Thou shalt," " Thou shalt not," hedges him round on every side, — now as moral obligation, and again as ceremonial or legal ordinance, — and becomes the bulwark of the faith through centuries of greatness, centuries of darkness and humiliation. Armed with this Word, as with the sword of the Most High, they go forth to conquer and overspread the land. Jehovah is always there, behind the scenes, the Deus ex Machina, their own special god, who has chosen them for his own special people, guiding and prompting them. It is always his right hand that doeth valiantly and is exalted when Israel triumphs, for he cares only for Israel. It is he who smites great kings, Israel's enemies, and slays them, for his mercy endureth forever, and who gives their land for an heritage to his people.

Amid a cloud of wars, Jehovah's sacred wars, with shadowy hosts and chieftains, the scattered clans unite, the kingdom forms, and we have the dawn of history. Jerusalem is founded, at once a stronghold and a sanctuary, and the temple built. The national and religious life grow as one growth, knitting themselves together and mutually strengthening and upholding one another. Then the splendours of Solomon's reign, the palace with royal state, and, above all, the ever-growing magnificence of the temple service, with more and more sumptuous rites and costly offerings, the priesthood, and all the paraphernalia of worship.

But the true greatness of Israel was never to consist in outward greatness, nor in the materialising of any of its ideas, either in the religious or the secu-

lar life, but wholly in the inner impulse
and activity, the spiritual impetus which
was now shaping itself into prophetism.
And here we strike the second chord,
that other source and spring of Israel's
life, which still yields living waters. In
Hebrew prophecy we have no crumbling
monument of perishable stone, the silent
witness of a past that is dead and gone,
but the quickening breath of the spirit
itself, the words that live and burn, the
something that is still alive and life-
giving, because it holds the soul of a
people, the spirit that cannot die.

It is difficult for us to realise at what
an early date this great movement had
its rise ; already a thousand years before
Christ we have the episode of Nathan
before David, pointing the parable and
laying his moral judgment upon the
king himself, — " Thou art the man."
And again, enveloped in legendary clouds,

the apocalyptic figure of Elijah, and the grand prophetic drama with its splendid accessories and scenery, — the whirlwind and the earthquake, and the still, small voice.

I have said that the true glory of Israel did not consist in any external and material embodying; and yet in a sense this was the stimulus and exciting cause, for it was in reaction against it that the Prophets uttered their ringing words and passionate appeal. Theirs was the clearer vision that pierced below the surface and penetrated to the hidden meaning, the moral and spiritual interpretation of the Law, in contrast with its outer sense. Thus their splendid outbursts : —

" I hate, I despise your feast days. . . . Though ye offer me your burnt offerings and your meat offerings, I will not accept them. . . . Take thou away

from me the noise of thy songs, for I
will not hear the melody of thy viols.
But let judgment run down as waters,
and righteousness as a mighty stream."

Throughout their history we find that
the Jews as a nation have been the " God-
intoxicated " race, intent upon the problem of understanding Him and His ways
with them, His rulings of their destiny.
With this idea, whether in a high form
or a low, in spiritual or material fashion,
their whole existence has been identified.
But it is the Prophets above all in whom
it has been concentrated and embodied
in its greatest intensity. For them but
one motive-power existed, but one source
and goal of action. In their ardent
souls, as in a burning glass, the thought
of Deity was centred, — a fire that con-
sumed them, a shining light for men.
To each one individually came the call,
the message, the direct revelation from
on high.

How lovely the word of Jeremiah :
"Then said I, Ah! Lord God, behold I
cannot speak, for I am a child. But the
Lord said unto me, Say not I am a child ;
for thou shalt go to all that I shall send
thee, and whatsoever I command thee
thou shalt speak."

And again the vision of Isaiah : "Woe
is me, for I am undone ; because I am a
man of unclean lips, . . . for mine eyes
have seen the King, the Lord of Hosts."
Then flew the seraph with the live coal
from off the altar and laid it upon the
prophet's lips, making him pure to speak.
"Also I heard the voice of the Lord,
saying, Whom shall I send and who will
go for us? Then said I, Here am I,
send me."

In the Hebrew writings we trace not
so much the development of a people
as of an idea, that constantly grows in
strength and purity. The petty, tribal

god, cruel and partisan, like the gods around him, becomes the universal and eternal God, who fills all time and space, all heaven and earth, and beside whom no other power exists. Throughout nature His will is law. His fiat goes forth, and the stars obey Him in their course, the wind and waves. " Fire and hail, snow and vapours, stormy wind fulfilling His word." " The lightnings do His bidding and say ' Here we are' when He commands them."

But not alone in the physical realm, still more is He the moral ruler of the universe; and here we come upon the core of the Hebrew conception, its true grandeur and originality, upon which the whole stress was laid, — namely, that it is only in the moral sphere, only as a moral being, that man can enter into relation with his Maker and the Maker of the universe, and come to any understanding of Him. "Canst thou by searching find out God? Canst thou find out the Almighty unto perfection? It is as high as heaven: what canst thou do? Deeper than hell: what canst thou know?"

Not through the finite, limited intellect, nor any outward sense-perception, but only through the inner moral sense, do these earnest teachers bid us seek God, who reveals Himself in the law which is at once human and divine, the voice of duty and of conscience, animating the soul of man. Like the stars, he, too, can obey; and then his righteousness will shine forth as the noonday sun, his going forth will be like the dawn.

It is this breath of the divine that vitalises the pages of the Hebrew prophets and their moral precepts. It is the blending of the two ideals, the complete and absolute identification of the moral and relig-

ious life, so that each can be interpreted
in terms of the other; the moral life
saturated and fed, sustained and sanc-
tified by the divine, the religious life
merely a divinely ordained morality, —
this it is that constitutes the essence
of their teachings, the unity and grand
simplicity of their ideal. The link was
never broken between the human and
divine, between conduct and its motive,
religion and morality, nor obscured by
any cloudy abstractions of theology or
metaphysics. Their God was a God
whom the people could understand, —
no mystic figure relegated to the skies,
but a very present power working upon
earth ; a personality very clear and distinct, — very human, one might almost
say, who mingled in human affairs,
whose word was swift and sure, and
whose path so plain to follow " that
wayfaring men, though fools, should not

err therein." What He required was no impossible ideal, but simply to do justice, to love mercy, and walk humbly before him. What He promised was : "Seek ye Me, and ye shall live."

How can one fail to be impressed by the heroic mould of these austere, impassioned souls, and by the richness of the soil that gave them birth at a time when spiritual thought had scarcely dawned upon the world! The Prophets were the "high lights" of Judaism ; but the light failed, the voices ceased, and prophetism died out. Was it only on account of the people's shortcomings, or was there not also inherent defect in itself ? In spite of its broad ethical and social basis, its seeming universality, it never became the religion of the masses, because in reality it is the religion of the few, the elect and chosen of God, who know and feel the beauty of His holiness. It did not hold, it could not touch the wayward and unrepentant ; its motive and appeal were not close, not searching enough to reach the unreached depths, the inmost core of living, and set free hidden springs. The Prophets were always denouncing, always protesting and inveighing against wickedness. Like rifts in the storm-cloud are the glimpses of tenderness and compassion, the promises, the vision of a God who will not always chide, whose anger will not last forever.

But what the people needed was something more penetrating and persuasive, or else something more congenial to their actual development at the time, — namely, some concrete and sensuous form in which Deity could be brought into life. Therefore the code was devised, or rather it evolved and grew like a natural growth out of the conditions and constitution of Judaism.

The Torah was literally the body of the Law, in which the spirit was encased as in a mummy shroud. It was the most subtle and elaborate scheme, the most ingenious mechanism ever contrived to weave together the human and divine into a method and polity of life that should be wholly sacramental, and so peculiarly adapted to the requirements and circumstances of the people for whom it was intended that, from this time forth, it made their destiny, and in a singular and fateful way preserved them, while it arrested their development.

In order that Israel should survive, should continue to exist at all in the midst of the ruins that were falling around it and the darkness upon which it was entering, it was necessary that this close, internal organisation, this mesh and network of law and practice, of regulated usage covering the most insignificant acts of life, knitting them together as with nerve and sinew, and invulnerable to any catastrophe from without, should take the place of all external prop and form of unity. The whole outer framework of life fell away. The kingdom perished, the temple fell, the people scattered. They ceased to be a nation, they ceased to be a church; and yet, indissolubly bound by these invisible chains, as fine as silk, as strong as iron, they presented an impenetrable front to the outside world, they became more intensely national, more exclusive and sectarian, more concentrated in their individuality than they had ever been before. The Talmud came to reinforce the Pentateuch, and rabbinism intensified Judaism, which thereby lost its power to expand, its claim to become a universal religion, and remained the prerogative of a peculiar people.

With fire and sword the Christian era
dawned for Israel. Jerusalem was be-
sieged, the temple fired, the holy Mount
in flames, and a million people perished,
—a fitting prelude to the long tragedy
that has not ended yet, the martyrdom
of eighteen centuries: death in every
form, by flood, by fire, and with every
torture that could be conceived, leaving
a track of blood through history; the
crucified of the nations; strangers and
wanderers in every age and every land,
calling no man friend and no spot home;
withal, the ignominy of the Ghetto, a
living death. Dark, pitiable, ignoble
destiny! Magnificent, heroic, unconquer-
able destiny, luminous with self-sacrifice,
unwritten heroism, devotion to an ideal,
a cause believed in, and a name held
sacred! But destiny still unsolved, martyrdom not yet swallowed up in victory.

In our modern, rushing days life

changes with such swiftness that it is difficult even to follow its rapid movement. During the last hundred years Judaism has undergone more modification than during the previous thousand years. The French Revolution sounded a note of freedom so loud, so clamorous, that it pierced the Ghetto walls and found its way to the imprisoned souls. The gates were thrown open, the light streamed in from outside, and the Jew entered the modern world. As if by enchantment, the spell which had bound him hand and foot, body and soul, was broken, and his mind and spirit, released from thrall, sprang into re-birth and vigour. Eager for life in every form and in every direction, with unused, pent-up vitality, he pressed to the front, and crowded the avenues where life was most crowded, thought and action most stimulated. And in order to this move-

ment, naturally and of necessity, he be-
gan to disengage himself from the toils
in which he was involved, to unwind
himself, so to speak, from fold after
fold of outworn and outlandish custom
and usages not alone irksome, but even
intolerable, and incompatible with any
but an immured and cloistered life.
Casting off the outer shell or skeleton,
which, like the bony covering of the
tortoise, serves as armour at the same
time that it impedes all movement and
progress as well as inner growth, Judaism thought to revert to its original
type, — the pure and simple monotheism
of the early days, the simple creed that
right is might, the simple law of justice
among men.

Divested of its spiritual mechanism,
absolutely without myth or dogma of
any kind, save the all-embracing unity
of God, taxing so little the credulity of

men, no religion seemed so fitted to withstand the storm and stress of modern thought, the doubt and scepticism of a critical and scientific age that has played such havoc with time-honoured creeds. And having rid himself, as he proudly believed, of his own superstitions, naturally the Jew had no inclination to adopt what he looked upon as the superstitions of others. He was still as much as ever the Jew, as far as ever removed from the Christian standpoint and outlook, the Christian philosophy and solution of life. Broad and tolerant as either side might consider itself, there was a fundamental disagreement and opposition, almost a different make-up, a different calibre and attitude of soul, fostered by centuries of mutual alienation and distrust. To be a Jew was still something special, something inherent, that did not depend upon any external conformity or non-conformity, any peculiar mode of life. The tremendous background of the past, of traditions and associations so entirely apart from those of the people among whom they dwelt, threw them into strong relief. They were a marked race always, upon whom an indelible stamp was set; a nation that cohered not as a political unit, but as a single family, through ties the most sacred, the most vital and intimate, of parent to child, of brother and sister, bound still more closely together through a common fate of suffering. And yet they were everywhere living among Christians, making part of Christian communities, and mixing freely among them for all the business of life, all material and temporal ends.

Thus the spiritual and secular life, which had been absolutely one with the Jew, grew apart in his own sphere, as well as in his intercourse with the Chris-

tians; the divorce was complete between
religion and the daily life. In his inmost consciousness, deep down below
the surface, he might be still a Jew, but
for the rest he would be a Gentile. The
Gentile world allured him, and the false
gods whom the nations around him
worshipped, — success, power, the pride
of life and of the intellect. He threw
himself full tilt into the arena where the
clash was loudest, the press thickest, the
struggle keenest to compete and out-
strip one another, which we moderns
call life. All his faculties were sharpened
to it, and in his eagerness he forgot his
proper birthright. He drifted away
from his spiritual bearings, and lost sight
of spiritual horizons. He, the man of
the past, became essentially the man of
to-day, with interest centred on the
present, the actual; with intellect set
free to grapple with the problems of the

hour, and solve them by its own unaided light. Liberal, progressive, humanitarian he might become, but always along human lines ; the link was gone with any larger, more satisfying, and comprehensive life. Religion had detached itself from life, not only in its trivial every-day concerns, but in its highest aims and aspirations. The something that the Hebrew prophets had, that made their moral teaching vital and luminous, was lacking, — the larger vision reaching out to the unseen, the abiding sense of an eternal will and purpose underlying human transient schemes, an eternal presence, transfusing all of life as with a hidden flame, so that love of country, love of right, love of man, were not alone human things, but also divine, because they were embraced and focussed in a single living unity, that was the love of God. How different now the cold,

abstract, and passive unity, the only
article of their faith now left to them,
that had no hold whatever, no touch
with life at any point, no kindling
power !

In what of positive and vital did their
Judaism consist ?   Were they not rather
Jews by negation, by opposition, non-
Christians, first and foremost ?   And
here was just the handle, just the grievance, for their enemies to seize upon.
Every charge would fit.   Behold the
Jew !   Behold one not ourselves, who
would be one of us !   Our masters, even,
who would wrest our prizes from us,
whose keen wits and clever fingers have
somehow touched the inner springs that
rule our world to-day and set its wheels
in motion !   Every cry could shape itself
against them, every class could take alarm,
and every prejudice go loose.   And hence
the Proteus form of anti-Semitism.

Wherever the social conditions are most unstable, the equilibrium most threatened and easily disturbed, in barbarous Russia, liberal France, and philosophic Germany, the problem is most acute; but there is no country now, civilised or uncivilised, where some echo of it has not reached; even in our own free-breathing America, some wave has come to die upon our shores.

And in view of such a situation, with such contingencies within us and without, how are we equipped, how are we prepared as Jews, to meet it and be true to our highest, largest destiny? What answer have we for ourselves and for the world in this, the trial hour of our faith, the crucial test of Judaism?

Each one of us must look into our own hearts and see what Judaism stands for in that inner shrine; what it holds that satisfies our deepest need, consoles and fortifies us, compensates for every sacrifice, every humiliation we may be called upon to endure, so that we can count it a glory, not a shame, to suffer. Will national or personal loyalty suffice for this when our personality is not touched, our nationality is merged? Will pride of family or race take away the sting, the stigma? Lo, we have turned the shield, and persecution becomes our opportunity. " Those that were in darkness, upon them the light hath shined."

What is the meaning of this exodus from Russia, from Poland, these long, black lines like funeral lines, crossing the frontiers or crushed within the pale, these " despised and rejected of men," emerging from their Ghettos, scarcely able to bear the light of day? Many of them will never see the Promised Land ; and for those who do, cruel will be the suffering before they enter, long and difficult will be the task and process of assimilation and regeneration. But for us, who stand upon the shore, in the full blessed light of freedom, and watch at last the ending of that weary pilgrimage through the centuries, how great the responsibility, how great the occasion, if only we can rise to it! Let us not think our duty ended when we have taken in the wanderers, given them food and shelter, and initiated them into the sharp daily struggle to exist, upon which we are all embarked; nor yet guarding their exclusiveness, when we leave them to their narrow rites and limiting observance, until, breaking free from these, they find themselves, like their emancipated brethren elsewhere, adrift on a blank sea of indifference and materialism.

If Judaism would be anything in the world to-day, it must be a spiritual force. Only then can it be true to its special mission, the spirit, not the letter of its truth. And as we have seen, it does not remain a spiritual force, when, holding itself aloof, it only shares the worldly life of those around it, and is brought only in contact with worldly influences.

Away, then, with all the Ghettos! and with spiritual isolation in every form, and let the " spirit blow where it listeth." The Jew must change his attitude before the world, and come into spiritual fellowship with those around him. We must cross the Rubicon, the blank page that separates the Old Testament from the New, and read with fresh eyes, fresh hearts, the life and teachings of the one whom the world calls Master. We shall not thereby leave our own soil. John, Paul, Jesus himself, — we can claim them all for our own. We do not want " missions " to convert us ; we cannot become Presbyterians, Episcopalians,

members of any dividing sect "teaching
for doctrines the opinions of men."
Christians as well as Jews need the
larger unity that shall embrace them
all, the unity of spirit, not of doctrine.

Mankind at large may not be ready for
a universal religion; but let the Jews, with
their prophetic instinct, their deep, spiritual insight, set the example and give the
ideal. The Jewish idea, broaden it as we
may, straiten it as we may, does not
contain all the truth. Neither the Law
nor the Prophets, the ceremonial nor the
moral code, covers the whole of that
mysterious experience we call life, and
that still greater mystery that in our
ignorance we call death. But the Law
fulfilled, which is Love, as "Christ
the Jew" taught and lived it, — love
as the very essence of all life, human
as well as divine, — brings a radiant
presence that transfigures life and death,

a new conception and explanation of our destiny.

But the world has not yet fathomed the secret of its redemption, and "salvation may yet again be of the Jews." Once again, by a supreme act of self-sacrifice, by voluntarily laying down that which they held to be their life, and which through all these darkened years they had guarded as their most sacred trust and treasure, can the Jews become the Messiah of the nations, lighting the fires that have been allowed to go out, and holding up the torch for all mankind. But this can only be by absorption and assimilation of the spiritual wealth of the world, not by denial and exclusion.

I should like to quote in this connection a few passages from the Hibbert Lectures of Claude Montefiore, a masterly exposition of Judaism. He says : —

"It is only now that this amazing

idealisation of the law is slowly breaking down, when the Pentateuch is being
estimated at its actual historic worth,
and subjected to the scalpel of a criticism
which disintegrates its unity and be-
reaves it of its supernatural glamour,
that Judaism will, I think, gradually
begin to feel the want of a dominant
and consistent doctrine, adequate and
comprehensive, soul-satisfying and ra-
tional, which can set forth and illumi-
nate in its entire compass the relation
of the individual to society and to God.
I am myself inclined to believe that,
from the words attributed in the Gospels
to Jesus, important elements toward the
formation of such a congruous body of
doctrine could well be chosen out, —
elements which would harmonise, de-
velop, and bring together the highest
religious teaching in the Old Testament
and the early rabbinical literature, and

5

which a prophetic though not a legal
Judaism, with full consistency and much
advantage, might adopt and cherish as
its own. . . . Some of the sayings as-
cribed to Jesus have sunk too deep into
the human heart — or shall I say into
the spiritual consciousness of civilised
mankind ? — to make it probable that
any religion which ignores or omits
them will exercise a considerable influence outside its own borders."

The times are full of signs. On every
side there is a call, a challenge, and awakening. Out of the heart of our materi-
alistic civilisation has come the cry of the
spirit hungering for its food, " the bread
without money and without price," the
bread which money cannot buy, and
" thirsting for the living waters, which if
a man drink he shall not thirst again."
What the world needs to-day, — not alone
the Jews, who have borne the yoke, but

the Christians, who bear Christ's name and persecute, and who have built up a civilisation so entirely at variance with the principles he taught, — what we all need, Gentiles and Jews alike, is not so much "a new body of doctrine," which Mr. Montefiore suggests, but a new spirit put into life, which will re-fashion it upon a nobler plan and consecrate it anew to higher purpose and ideals. Science has done its work, clearing away the dead wood of ignorance and superstition, enlarging the vision and opening out the path. It is for religion now to fill with spirit and with life the facts that knowledge gives us, to breathe a living soul into the universe.

"Return unto me, and I will return unto you, saith the Lord of Hosts." "All we, like sheep, have gone astray." Christians and Jews alike have turned from the true path, worshipping upon the high places and under every green tree, falling down before idols of gold and silver, and making graven images of every earthly and every heavenly thing.

Thus have we builded a kingdom wholly of the earth, solid and stately to the eye of sense, but hollow and honey-combed with falsehood, and whose foundations are so insecure that they tremble at every earthly shock, every attempt at readjustment; and we half expect to see the brilliant pageant crumble before our sight, and disappear like the unsubstantial fabric of a dream.

Christians and Jews alike, "Have we not all one Father; hath not one God created us?" Remember to what you are called, you who claim belief in a living God who is a Spirit, and who therefore must be "worshipped in spirit and in truth," — not with vain forms and meaningless service, nor yet in the world's glittering shapes, the work of men's hands or brains; but in the ever-growing, ever-deepening love and knowledge of His truth, and its showing forth to men.

Once more let the Holy Spirit descend and dwell among you in your life to-day, as it did upon your holy men, your prophets of the olden times, lighting the world, as it did for them, with that radiance of the skies. And so make known the faith that is in you; "for by their fruits ye shall know them."

September, 1893.

JUDAISM, OLD AND NEW.

"EPUR si muove." The world moves, and there is ever a new dawn breaking for those whose eyes are turned toward the light. A few years ago the life of the Jew was a sealed book to most of his contemporaries. Here and there a solitary figure, an exceptional character in real life or in fiction, stood out in bold and exaggerated relief, generally unrelated or falsely related to its surroundings, and therefore conveying but little idea of the truth.

To-day we have almost a new Jewish literature of our own, springing up in our midst, dealing not with foreign conditions and circumstance, but with the facts as they are here and now among us; depicting not the historic Jew of the past, the ideal and impossible Jew of the imagination, but the real and actual Jew of the present, the modern Jew whose name is Legion — no less than ever, perhaps, an enigmatic figure, as he moves everywhere among his fellow-men, in the crowd and yet not quite of it; or as he stands apart, wrapped in strange guise and custom, and speaking a language which the world of to-day does not understand. He who runs may read, and, indeed, there is no excuse, no escape for the modern Jew of even the most ordinary stamp and culture. He *must* know the status of his people, the problems that beset them; and if he does, he cannot fail to bring whatever heart or brain he has to try to understand and solve them.

For surely no people are confronted

by so singular a destiny, past, present, and to come. Never was there a situation so complicated, with elements so diverse and contradictory, to be fused, reconciled, and assimilated: not one nation, but every nation, and generally the outcast and rejected of that nation; aliens wherever they tread, wherever they seek to find a home, even among their own race, since there is no strong hand to guide and gather them in, no true leadership, no adequate idea to rally round, no single goal or purpose to bind and knit together.

In "The Children of the Ghetto, The Grandchildren of the Ghetto," Mr. Zangwill tells the story for us with dramatic force and realism. Sweeping, as he does, the whole field of vision, the social scale from bottom upward, he gives, as it were, an epitome of Jewish life and history; so that it is to his vivid pages, almost rather than to life itself, that we would turn for the bird's-eye view in which no detail is lost, the broad survey of his subject, the bold, free handling, and yet the human sympathy and insight. With master hand he throws the flash-light and illuminates the canvas for us, — a great *tableau vivant*, a moving panorama, crowded with figures of every age and clime, and touched with every shade of colour, light and darkness. The patriarch of hoary, long-forgotten days, the mediæval shapes, still muffled and draped with the past, are there; the bourgeois and the Philistine of to-day, the idealist, the sad-eyed, and the hopeful dreamer, the visionary whose ardent gaze is fastened on a vision among the clouds, or wanders and is lost in far-away horizons that escape and elude him.

It is the whole drama of Israel that is always repeating itself, for the reason that the past as well as the present is an actuality; the old types survive and are reproduced, while new ones are being born. Thus the strange contrasts and juxtapositions, the anomalies, we might almost say, the fatality of Judaism. For the outer life is but the reflection of the inner; here also the same chaos reigns, the same lack of unity and coherence, the perpetual clash and conflict always to be renewed, until, if ever, we reach an idea large enough to reconcile the old and new, the present with the past.

As Mr. Zangwill paints it (and he paints it truly), Judaism seems but a tragic masquerade, a kaleidoscope of shifting, many-coloured views. His characters are swayed back and forth: now carried forward by a wave of aspiration and progress, and again swept backward by a still stronger tide that they cannot resist. We are wandering in the wilder-

ness again; here and there a mirage, a
dream of the past, a dream of the future,
as of light breaking through the clouds,
but the darkness gathers and settles
again. We close the book with a deep
sense of tragedy and unrest, of lives
blighted and bewildered, tossed upon a
sea of doubts and perplexities, of unsolved destiny; and we ask ourselves: Is
this, then, the last word of our Judaism?
Is it a failure, a mistake, a " misfortune,"
as Heine puts it; " a forlorn hope, an
impossibility," as Mr. Zangwill's heroine,
Esther Ansell, mournfully concludes? —
and she knew whereof she spoke. Must
it hang henceforth on two horns of a
dilemma, unable to save, unable to lose
itself; or else, moving in a circle, must
it endlessly revolve upon itself?

But before even attempting to give
an answer to these questions, let us
glance at some other books before us.

In " Joseph Zalmonah," Edward King
deals with the social and economic problem, the horrors of the sweating system,
the overstocked labour market, and the
special phases connected with the influx
of Russian and Polish immigration, — in
a word, the " bondage" of the wretched
exiles in the land of promise, which they
find to their cost " is not a land of per-
formance."   Step by step he traces the
course of the hapless refugee back to
Russia, escaping from the Pale, and flee-
ing in the dark winter night across the
bridge into Germany; the emigrant ship
arriving in New York; the little crowd of
exiles on the lower deck, standing with
uncovered head, outstretched arms, and
glistening eyes to greet the Statue of
Liberty, " the mighty symbol of freedom
and refuge from tyranny; " the dreams,
the hopes, and then, alas! the cruel
deceptions, the bitter reality, " the sick-

ening search for work, the wretched lodg-
ings, the repulsive food, the failure to
find anything to do;" "Misery Market,"
where the last treasure disappears,—the
gold watch, the fur coat and cap, — and,
finally, the sweaters' hell, where the
grinding wheel of Sisyphus eternally re-
volves, and the wretched toiler faints and
drops by the way.

I would not here rehearse the ghastly
scenes, the pitiful details, but refer the
reader to Mr. King's graphic pages if he
would study this woful aspect of our
modern civilisation. Throughout the
book the author has skilfully contrived
to keep the local colour and traits, the
peculiar stamp of Orientalism; and he
opens for us so curious a bit of New
York life, something so altogether unique
and unexpected, that it is difficult for us
to realise unless we have already made
ourselves familiar with it. His descrip-

tions are drawn from the life, within a stone's throw of our own homes, in the heart of our own city; and yet they seem as far removed as the East is from the West, as foreign and absolutely un-American as anything that could be met with, the world over. It is all a sort of " jargon " of sights and sounds and colours, — the Hebrew signs and letters on the houses, the motley crowd, the motley wares spread everywhere upon the sidewalk, the market, the theatre, — all making a nondescript medley and conglomerate, as though an unknown stratum of the earth had come to obtrude and superimpose itself upon the surface.

Again we feel like crying out : " How long, O Lord, how long ? " But we know that in a twinkling, before a generation shall have passed away, in less than a twelvemonth indeed, the children of these outcasts have been taught to speak

English and prepared for the public schools. The American flag has been explained to them, and, like a prayer, each morning they have offered their allegiance. And we realise that for some of these at least new ideas are being born, new conditions are being created, that will sweep away the old landmarks more effectually than flood or fire, or time or space.

Quite a different note, and yet no less deep and true a one, is struck in the modest, unpretending little volume, almost child-like in its simplicity, "Other Things Being Equal," by Emma Wolf. We have here the problem that is left when all other problems are solved, all other differences and obstacles have been set aside. It is the final, ultimate step— shall we say the solution? The Jew and the Christian meet on absolutely equal terms. On neither side is any disparity recognised. Mentally, morally, socially, the man and the woman are equally matched. "Religiously they hold the same broad love for God and man." Shall they intermarry? And now, out of its last stronghold, arises the ghost of the past, — not a stern, pitiless, and forbidding figure, but a gentle, dear, and good old man, a most loving and beloved father, who, with broken heart and broken voice, tells his daughter: "No, my child, I cannot consent, and yet I shall not withhold. I do most solemnly and seriously object, . . . but trust me, dear, it is through no lack of love for you. Do not consider me; forget, if you will, all I have said. . . . The door is open; you can pass through without my hand."

The charm and pathos of the book, as well as its originality, consist in the fact that it is love, and always love, that conquers every time. The author has taken for her motto: " And now abideth faith, hope, and love, these three: but the greatest of these is love." Ruth Levice gives up her lover, not from a sense of duty, but because she loves her father better than herself, or than her lover, who had become part of herself. She writes to Dr. Kemp: —

" Only *I* am causing this separation; no one else could or would. Do not blame my father; if he were to see me writing thus he would beg me to desist; he would think I am sacrificing my happiness for him. . . . I am no Jephthah's daughter; he wants no sacrifice, and I make none. Duty, the hardest word to learn, is not leading me. . . . Let me say it now — I could never be happy with you."

Her father's arguments have not convinced her. She stands just where she stood before, high above all prejudice and narrowness of view; but no convictions of her own, no dream of happiness, can outweigh the knowledge of her father's broken life, the picture of his stooping form as he turns from her, bent as beneath the burden of the past. Bravely and resolutely she takes up her life, doing nothing by halves, determined at any cost to make her father happy. But the struggle tells, and the eyes of love cannot be deceived. Her father realises the sacrifice that has been made and the motive for it, all the love and anguish of the struggle; and with the knowledge comes a higher vision, a deeper and larger perception than he had had before. He, too, rises out of self, out of views that were personal and perhaps peculiar, and trusts the larger love that now is guiding him. He acknowledges his mistake. He says : —

"I stood convicted. I was in the position of a blind fool who, with a beautiful picture before him, fastens his critical, condemning gaze upon a rusting nail in the wall behind, a nail even now loosened, and which in another generation will be displaced."

As the blue sky arches over all alike, he argues, high and low, rich and poor, great and small, so does the all-encompassing love of God — the same God — hold all of us alike, Jew and Christian, believer and unbeliever. Differences of belief, like all other differences, are human, not divine — matters of human opinion. In God's sight, God's love, all are one, all are His children, and therefore brothers. What are we, who in our erring human judgment should try to put asunder those whom God hath truly joined together in soul and spirit, so that no human circumstance or difference has

power to part them? And with this conviction, Mr. Levice gives his daughter to
the man she loves.

It is impossible in a brief review to
give an idea of the rare tenderness and
pathos with which the subject is treated,
even in its minor details and characters.
There is a hint, a touch of something so
unusual in the book that we are tempted
to exclaim: "Ah, yes, but it is not true
to life!" And neither is it; but that is
because life, as we most of us live it, is
not true to itself, its best self, its highest
possibilities and ideals, the faith, the
hope, the love that we were meant to
live by.

And it is just here that the little volume gives the keynote of what one would
like to say. After all, what is the vital
question to-day, as it has always been,
through all time and all vicissitudes, with
which we Jews have to deal? Is it not

now as it has ever been, — how to keep
the Faith ? Throughout the centuries,
what endless martyrdom, what countless
sacrifices for this ! And now that the
martyrdom has ceased, that the clouds
seem to lift, and we advance from slavery
into freedom, from darkness into light,
the question, so far from growing clearer,
becomes an increasingly difficult one.

We stand upon the threshold of we
know not what, — unable to go backward,
not daring to go forward. The future
beckons us on with promise of wider,
freer life, unchecked growth and scope,
broad, unhampered human and spiritual
fellowship. The past holds us with invincible weight. " Deny me, and you deny
yourself," it says; " your very life, all
that makes you what you are." The
blood of martyrs seems to cry to us:
" Would you be faithless, then, to us,
and have we died in vain ? "

And whence come these questionings, this doubt and division of soul? Surely from lack of faith and vision, rather than from true loyalty and conviction. Not in vain will be that martyrdom when it has taught us to be faithful as those martyrs were, and when we have, as they had, a faith of our own to be true to; when we are ready to trust and follow it wherever it may lead, to deny self and offer up life for its sake. But we have lost the faith, not merely in the narrow, historic sense, not alone in allegiance to the past, in outward conformity to external rites and inherited usage, but as an inward, quickening power, a source of our spiritual life and action, a vision of something that makes life holy, beautiful, and blessed, whatever martyrdom we may be called upon to endure, whatever sacrifice we may be called upon to make.

And when we read it aright, the story of our people means, above all else, this faith, a perfect trust and confidence in the leading and purpose of the Most High, whatever that leading and purpose may be, and whether or not we understand it. "Though He slay me, yet will I trust in Him." Did Abraham hesitate when God bade him leave his Mesopotamian home and go, " he knew not whither," to found a new home, a new nation ? Did Moses heed the murmurs and discontent of those who would have returned to bondage in Egypt rather than be led through the wilderness ?

Whether or not we have the prophetic vision, whether or not we see and understand the promise beyond, we can be faithful still, now that we find ourselves on the verge of a larger deliverance than ever before. They are the faithless who would lag behind.

" New occasions teach new duties ;
　　Time makes ancient good uncouth.
They must upward still and onward
　　Who would keep abreast of truth.
Lo! before us gleam the camp fires!
　　We, ourselves, must pilgrims be,

.　　　.　　　.　　　.　　　.

Nor attempt the Future's portal,
　　With the Past's blood-rusted key."

It is the task of Judaism to be up and doing, alert and ready to receive, not passively accepting what has been handed down, nor yet watching the smouldering fires of a lingering sacrifice. Let us take our Judaism fearlessly out into the world, to be put to any test, but, above all, freely to be used, not in its own service, but in the service of the God in whom it believes, the universal Father of all, and, therefore, in the world's highest service. And in order to do this, first and foremost we must be rid of self, of this intense pre-occupation to survive in any form, as race or creed or nation, this desperate struggle to exist in name, if nothing else. For herein lies our whole problem, our whole temptation, — not in the world around us, but in ourselves. What would we think of the soldier who offered to serve his country, but who would only go into battle on condition that his own life should be saved?

"Ah, but," I hear you exclaim, "that is a very different thing. We too would be willing to sacrifice our life; but we are not willing to sacrifice our principles, our deepest convictions, which are dearer to us than life." And I do not hesitate to answer (at least to those who have passed out of the dark ages of superstition and useless, orthodox formalism), you are not called upon to sacrifice your deepest principles and convictions; on the contrary, you are summoned to be true to them by casting down the barriers that prevent their fullest exercise and freedom in the widest relation with your fellow-men. Search well your own heart, and perhaps you will find that, once placing yourself in this attitude, throwing off the heavy weight of the past, this dead self that clings to you, you will be born again, into your larger heritage; you will no longer be conscious of difference and separation; you will be one with your brother, the liberal Christian who has likewise come out of the narrowness of his creeds and doctrine into the same freedom as you have, — the glorious freedom of the sons of God, the God of Abraham, Isaac, and Jacob: yes, but the God of the living, not of the dead. Creeds are everywhere falling and being disintegrated, losing their hard-and-fast consistency in order that the truth that has been encased in them shall be set free, the light of the spirit shall shine out like a star. Christianity as a sect

or creed has no compelling force for
Judaism. The Inquisition could not
make Christians of us, nor can all the
mild but zealous efforts of the Presbyterians ever make a single honest convert.

That which alone has power supremely
to attract is the divine-human life, of
which the type has been given to the
world by a Jew. And by the divine-
human life I mean the life which through
every human experience keeps sight and
touch of the divine, — a life lived always
in conscious relation with infinite and
eternal things, in personal union and
communion with a Being that compre-
hends and transcends our own, and therefore a life of sublime trust and assurance,
of loving obedience, and of immortal
promise and hope. And the secret of
that life, the truth which it reads into
the world, through every contradiction
and obstruction of human circumstance,

every manifestation of human weakness, human sorrow and sin, is the truth of love, — of an infinite and eternal Love transcending human imperfections, a divine Heart that reveals itself in answering love to our human heart and human needs.

And is not such a life of the very essence of Judaism, you ask? And I answer: It may be, but not while you limit and circumscribe your Judaism as you do, making of it a fetich, a history and tradition instead of an active, living principle, a visible embodiment of the truth; not while you draw about yourselves the lines of a peculiar and chosen people that isolate you and forbid you from entering into the closest human ties with the people around you; not while you imprison yourselves in the past, as in a Ghetto from whence you refuse to emerge; or, mounting upon your watch-towers, as the Mohammedan does upon his, proclaim from everlasting to everlasting the unity of your God. Come down from your watch-towers, come out of your Ghettos, and bear witness to that unity in the world to-day, not as an abstract, metaphysical truth, but in spirit and in deed.

But again you will protest: "Surely we Jews, of all people, *are* in the world to-day, pressing everywhere to the front, or midmost in the thick of the struggle. See how we crowd the universities, fill the high places, and carry off the honours, following, leading everywhere among the great Powers that be. What other nation, crushed as we have been for centuries under the iron weight of Christendom, persecuted, down-trodden, and oppressed, and even yet under the shadow of our dungeon walls, could so rebound, so spring into life ready-armed for every emergency?"

Ah, then, is this all the Ghetto could teach us, — to fight the world's fight, to win in the world's race? Can we find no deeper purpose, no higher leading, no holier consecration in that martyrdom? Have we not kept alive and burning all these tragic years the perpetual lamp? Have we not guarded like a jewel in the dark, or, still more, like a precious seed buried in the earth, the sacred trust and treasure of the spiritual life, that should shine out now before all men, should burst into splendid flower and fruit as soon as it comes into the light of day? And does it so shine out? Has our Judaism, whether orthodox or liberal, blossomed so before the world? Are we the leaders of the religious and spiritual thought of the day?

In so far as we take part in it, are we not chiefly concerned with our own survival, our continued existence as a distinct element and factor? On the one hand, do we not clutch desperately the dry husks that we hold in our grasp, of external rites and devitalised formulæ, calling them bread for hungry souls; or else letting these go and casting them aside, do we not see our Judaism scattered to the winds, so that no man knows how to gather it?

Let us not be deceived. We cannot save our Judaism in any narrow, in any broad sense even, unless we lose it, by merging and adding to it that which will make it no longer Judaism, because it is something that the whole world claims, and therefore cannot be the exclusive prerogative of Judaism, — in other words, by entering into the larger, spiritual life which makes no conditions, no restrictions necessary; draws no boundary lines, no arbitrary and external distinctions of race and creed; sets up no barriers between

man and man, between man and God;
but reaches out in perfect freedom, perfect oneness with man, to perfect oneness with God.

But, once again, you will say : " Is
it not more often the Christians who
draw the line and set up the barriers;
who despise and persecute, so that in
self-defence we draw back upon ourselves;
who, when we hold out our hand, refuse
to take it?" That may be; and yet I
think we can do better than make these
our guide. Moreover, we shall always
find that for this there are special and
local causes, varying in nature and intensity, according to our own particular
condition and the condition of the country in which we dwell, but not necessarily radical and inherent in the people
around us, unless we make them so, by
insisting upon them in ourselves. We
must not forget the uncompromising

attitude which, for centuries long, the
Jew and the Christian have held in regard to one another, and which cannot
at once be done away with on either side.
We have stood too long in mutual distrust and hostility; our own race-features
have become too strongly emphasised.
We are largely foreigners to the people
among whom we live, and even those
of us who are acclimatised still bear
traces of our foreign origin.

Under these circumstances we cannot
expect to come at once into complete
understanding and accord. We can
never expect it, if, while apparently
freely mixing at the surface, we remain
apart at the core, covertly trying to keep
our own peculiarities and aloofness. We
must cultivate and grow into perfect freedom and fellowship, — slowly and laboriously, perhaps, for the task is a difficult
one, requiring infinite patience and for-

bearance, infinite tact and tenderness among ourselves as well as in our dealings with the Christians. Our own people must be gently raised and lifted, helped according to their individual needs, spiritual as well as material, and according to their capacity to receive, not knowing perhaps the goal to which they tend.

But those of us who have caught sight of the goal must never lose it from view, but must walk on, according to our faith and vision of the larger hope and promise, the complete deliverance, which is as essentially the Jewish as it is the Christian ideal, because it means the absolute unity, not alone the unity of God with Himself, one God as opposed to many gods, — a purely intellectual or mathematical axiom, — but the unity of God with us, a vitalising principle, a union as of life with its source, of parent with child ; a universal love that folds us round

with rest and tenderness, making our
human relations spiritual, our spiritual
relations almost human in that sense of
warmth and closeness that is so often
lacking. We can still repeat our creed :
"Hear, O Israel, — and hear all the
world besides, — the Lord our God, the
Lord is one," — one with us, with all of
us, Jews and Christians alike. For we
have taken into it an element that shall
so deepen and enlarge it as forever to
redeem it from self and every form of
selfishness, all possibility of narrowness
and sectarianism. No longer shutting
itself in, nor shutting any out, on the
contrary, it will welcome all with, "Come
unto me, whatever sect, whatever race,
whatever creed, for in my larger love,
my larger faith, all sects, all creeds are
one."

Each of us has our special part, our
special work to do, which we cannot

shirk, even if we would, for it is forced upon us. To the most indifferent of us it must mean something for our good or ill, our weal or woe, that we are born Jews, into just these conditions in which we find ourselves, to work through them, if we can, into still higher conditions. We all stand at different points along the line, with some above us, some below, to help and to be helped. Judaism is to each of us a personal factor, an individual problem, as well as a large race-question, to be solved individually as well as collectively, — a problem as old as the world, which will be older yet before it is solved. But if we see any light, we need not despair. We can believe, we can hope and trust, and, above all, we can serve. " For now abideth faith, hope, and love, these three; but the greatest of these is love."

February, 1894.

THE CLAIM OF JUDAISM.

THAT history repeats itself is a truism with which we are all familiar; that we must read history backward is a fact of which we are again and again reminded in dealing with the Jewish question and trying to throw any light upon the problem. We open the second volume of Graetz's History and read as follows : —

"The wider view which had been gained into the various relations of life, the advance out of the narrow circle of tradition and inherited customs, produced schism and separation amongst the Judæans. . . . Thus, there arose a division among the pious" (viz., the Pharisees and

Sadducees). " The Pharisees can only be
called a party figuratively and by way of
distinction, . . . for the mass of the
nation was inclined to Phariseeism, and
it was only in the national leaders that
its peculiarities became marked. . . . As
expounders of the law, the Pharisees
formed the learned body of the nation.
Their opinions were framed, their actions
governed by one cardinal principle, —
the necessity of preserving Judaism.
The individual and the state were to be
ruled alike by the laws and customs of
their fathers. . . . From this, the Pharisees' view of life, the rival opinion of the
Sadducees diverged. . . . This party of
the Sadducees, so sharply opposed to the
Pharisees, . . . was composed of the Judæan aristocracy . . . who had acquired
wealth and authority at home, or who
had returned from foreign embassies, all
having gained, from closer intercourse

with the outer world and other lands,
freer thought and more worldly views.
The national interests of the Judæan community were placed by the Sadducees
above the Law. . . . As experienced men
of the world they felt that . . . man
must not allow himself to be kept back
by religious scruples from forming political alliances, . . . although by so doing
he must inevitably infringe some of the
injunctions of his religion."

Making exception of certain political
aspects, or rather substituting financial
and mercantile interests in place of national considerations, we have the Jewish
situation as it stands to-day, a picture of
our modern Jewish society. We seem to
be reading a page of contemporaneous
Jewish history. In reality, we are reading of events that transpired and of a
state of things that existed one hundred
and thirty-five years before Christ. For

us Jews time has stood still. The pen-
dulum has swayed backward and forward,
but the dial hands have not moved. Two
thousand years have rolled by, with their
endless change upon change; the storm of
modern life has swept over us; we are
living in a new world, in the midst of
undreamed-of circumstance and conditions, — and we are still disputing in the
synagogues, debating along precisely the
old lines, the old points of law, of orthodox
and unorthodox, the technicalities of usage
and belief, the *sine qua non* of survival.

In a word, we are still Pharisees and
Sadducees, rival sects, intent upon our
own salvation, and divided among ourselves : those of us who would keep the
Law to the letter in order to survive, and
those of us who would break it and still
survive, — the worldly-wise in our own
generation, who would relax and infringe
for worldly purpose and convenience,

while still keeping sacred and intact the distinction and prerogative of race. We have not changed our point of view in any direction; our destiny has not enlarged, our spiritual horizon has not widened. The banner that we hold aloft is " Self ": self-defence, self-preservation are our watchwords always. We beat the air, we fight with ghosts and shadows; and behind us Judaism looms up, stony and unmoved, a great monument of the past, a Sphynx half-buried in the desert sand of arid rites and customs, hoary and majestic with age, but dumb, enigmatic, with sealed eyes and lips that have no answer for our present urgent need, our problem of to-day.

But the hour has struck. The Sphynx must give her secret to the world, for the world is waiting, the world demands a solution.

From within and from without, the

question is pressing upon us. Literature
is flooded with it. The Christians, even
more than the Jews, are forcing us to
define and declare our position, to make
it clear just where we stand and what we
stand for, — not only among ourselves as
Jews, but in relation to the world at
large, to the Christians themselves, the
outside community in which we dwell, of
which we form a part, of which we never
truly form a part. On the one side, we
have anti-Semitism in one form or another, whether covert and disguised, or
else open, pronounced, and aggressive,
and breaking out where we had not
expected; on the part of the Jews, we
have defence, apology, recrimination,
but, above all, justification, — justification
without end, insistence and reiteration of
their own peculiar claim and service, their
plea for recognition and for justice that
is denied them. It may well be that the

attitude of the Christian is even more blameworthy than our own, but with this we are not for the moment concerned. For any one who has at heart the true dignity of the race, the real grandeur of their achievement, it is our own point of view that is of far graver import.

In view of the situation, is it not time that the strife of sects should cease, and party warfare have an end, in order that we may come to some better understanding among ourselves, some deeper reason for the faith that is in us, some larger answer, some truth more vital and more sacred to ourselves and to humanity than whether or not we keep the Mosaic Law, whether or not we merge as one people with the people around us, — a truth larger and deeper than sect or race, binding together even as one sect and race all who may hold it in common, God's chosen people everywhere? Failing this, are we doomed perpetually to revolve in the small and narrow circle of our own race-questions, our own peculiar interests, inevitably shut out by our own restrictions and limitations from that freedom and equality of intercourse that alone can insure harmony and good-will among men? Everywhere is the anomaly of our situation made apparent to us; again and again we are obliged to face it. And the secret of that anomaly lies, not in the people around us, as we so often suppose, but in ourselves, deep below any surface-difference or opposition, in the very heart of Judaism itself. Let us first consider the claim as put forth by its leaders and exponents, which may thus be formulated.

Judaism, in its ultimate destiny, in its essence and its spirit, is a universal religion, — the religion of humanity when humanity shall have grown to its full stature, the religion of the world when the world shall be capable of grasping and realising its lofty ideals.

Judaism in its actuality, in its very constitution, as we know it to-day, as we have known it through all time, in its spirit and its form, is the religion of particularism, the religion of a peculiar people, chosen and set apart; a peculiar code especially devised with the sole end and aim of separation as the very basis and condition of existence.

And in order that this particular may become the universal, what are we bidden to do? To intrench ourselves in the particular; to remain the peculiar people, the peculiar sect, if we would not incur the guilt of moral cowardice and suicide, the penalty of moral death. In order to teach our universal truth, our lofty ideals to the world, we must remain aloof from the world except for purposes that have no bearing upon this universal truth; we must carefully guard our sacred idea from intrusion or even contact with other sacred ideas; we must read no sacred books but our own; we must preach unity, and we must practise the most rigid exclusion, the most uncompromising separation the world has ever known. There shall be no marrying nor giving in marriage, either of the human or the spiritual. Soul shall not meet soul, life shall not be added unto life, because we are shut off from the soul-life of the community in which we dwell. We are one in the body, so to speak, — that is to say, for temporal purpose and convenience, — but in spirit we are wide asunder.

And I ask, Can such a union ever prove blessed, or beautiful, or happy? Must it not always be subject to the jars and friction to which we so constantly see ourselves exposed, to hopeless contradiction and misunderstanding? If, as we claim, we have the world's truth in our keeping, shall we therefore keep it for ourselves? Were it not larger, wiser, grander to give it to the world at the cost of any personal sacrifice to ourselves; to make the great renunciation, to die to self, to the particular, as people, race, or individual, in order that we may live to the universal, the larger life and ideal, the deeper purpose of humanity; to lose our life if thereby we might save it, by setting free the truth that is our life, and making known as never before the Unity of God, the universal Father, and the common brotherhood of man?

But it is just here that the fallacy lies, the paradox, that is deeper than any question of expediency, of whether or not we are comfortable among the nations, and amid our surroundings and circum-

stance. It lies in our belief, our clinging
to the idea that Judaism *is* the universal
religion, that it ever can or will adapt itself to the needs of men of every race, men
who have not inherited it in the blood.
Our mistake lies in supposing that it,
and it alone, contains the whole truth,
the absolute truth, and nothing but the
truth, the salvation of all mankind ; that
before it, was no truth, and that since, no
new truth has come into the world, no new
sacred principle or method of life, and,
therefore, nothing shall be added thereto
nor taken therefrom ; that in the matter
of spiritual or religious truth we Jews
have everything to teach and nothing to
learn, because Judaism holds the essence
of all that is good in the world; that
whatever in Christianity is not Judaism
is paganism ; that whatever Jesus taught
that Hillel had not taught before him is
nought, and worse than nought ; that

finally, in the Mosaic code and the
moral law, the reign of justice upon
earth, is contained all the spiritual un-
foldment, the sacred revealing, all the
help and leading that we need.

But we forget that even in Biblical
times, when Judaism shone out in its
greatest splendour, its moral supremacy
among the nations, it made no such claim
as this of perfection; it was always a
prophetic religion, a religion of promise
that pointed somewhere, somehow to a
fulfilment, a deliverance, a mysterious
coming — of a person, a kingdom — that
should complete and establish it upon
earth. Already in those far distant days
there was a lack felt, there was a link
wanting, a something that should bind
men close to God, a way of holiness, a
path whereby to approach, whereby to
bring Him near "that sitteth upon the
circle of the earth, and the inhabitants

thereof are as grasshoppers." Hence the
ceremonial code, with all its mechanical
contrivance to wrap God's presence round
the trivial, common things of daily life,
literally to nail Him on the doorposts, to
bind Him as frontlets upon brow and
arms, and knit Him upon the fringes of
the garments. And hence, above all,
the moral code, making known the terms
and the conditions of man's relation with
his Maker.

But even then men already dimly
felt that the moral law does not suffice,
does not necessarily bring us close to
God. On the contrary, it may estrange
us from Him by raising that terrible consciousness of sin, of the wide gap between
the human and the divine, between our
poor righteousness and His perfection,
not to be bridged over by any effort on
our part. Or, again, it may arouse that
false self-righteousness and spiritual pride,

so sure of itself, so confident in its own strength and sight, which is even further removed from God than weak human sinning. And so David, the man who sinned, was the man near God's heart, and, according to Isaiah, "Who is blind as he that is perfect, and blind as the Lord's servant?"

For there is a deeper, truer vision yet to be attained that brings to light the hidden, secret things of God's love and wisdom, rather than man's imperfect judgment, his paltry verdict of righteous and unrighteous; there is a more spiritual perception than that revealed by the moral law, for it comes from a more intimate sense of dependence, a closer communion, nay, an absolute oneness of spirit with Spirit, which cannot be severed by any weakness or error of the flesh.

But we Jews are not willing thus to transcend the Law and the Prophets, to accept the absolute and unconditioned unity of God with all His creatures. We still cling to our separateness in the inner as well as the outer life, trying in vain to make ourselves one with Him through outward rule and practice, through works, not faith; in what we do, rather than what we are.

And so it happens almost of necessity that when the framework of the rabbinical law falls away, for the most part we are left without God in our lives. We lose the sense of divine things even in the crude, realistic, and anthropomorphic way in which we once possessed it, — the touch of the spirit, — and, therefore, our spiritual life becomes barren and exhausted. We remain an ethical people, but we cease to be a religious people. Once a year perhaps, on the occasion of a great and solemn festival, we give up our business and wander to the syna-

gogue, listen to the chants and the sacred
intoning that carry us back among the
dead, into the dim vista of the past, and
go home satisfied that we are still Jews
at heart, in sentiment and association,
thankful that we are not as other men,
but that we can so easily leave superstition behind us, and content to have no
other link with our people and with God.

I have said that the present situation
was analogous with the past. In a sense
this is true, and in a sense the position
of the modern Jew is different from anything that has gone before ; for the conditions of modern society are so entirely
different. Everything is so fluent, plas-
tic, and changing from moment to moment ; everything goes at so quick a
pace, circulates so widely, freely, and rap-
idly. Thought is so active and alert, life
is at such high pressure and such close
pressure everywhere, that the Jew, even

more than others, keen and sensitive to these influences, is caught up and whirled along in the great stream of physical forces. He finds more and more difficulty in conforming to the exigencies of his religion, so that only an ever-diminishing number are willing to make the sacrifices imposed upon them. But he drifts with the tide, enjoying to the full, the play and freedom of long unused activities, the stimulus and excitement of the struggle, until a stern voice recalls him to himself. In the midst of the great, rushing, inexorable present that will not wait, but hurries him along, rises the great, fixed, inexorable past that bids him halt: "Thus far, and no farther. Thou canst not if thou wouldst be free. Look back! four thousand years! over the ruins of empire, the tombs of nations, the rise and fall of false faiths and perishable gods. There never was a time when

Israel did not exist. Shall Israel cease
to exist with thee?" A solemn call, and
we Jews must feel it so. We cannot
make the choice lightly, or for any slight
or worldly cause. Above all, we cannot
drift, we cannot shirk our destiny. We
must meet and face it, whatever it bring,
whatever it take away. But let us be
sure we hear the voice aright. Let us
listen, not to the voice of tradition and
authority, of human circumstance and
history, of human glory and survival,
not to the call of the Scribes and the
Pharisees, but to the voice of the
Prophets, the men of vision who proclaimed the eternal, the everlasting
Idea, yet to be attained, yet to be fulfilled, where others saw only the imperfect human fulfilment.

Let us not be deceived. It is not
enough merely to survive. The test of
an ideal, its true vitality, consists not in

survival, but in its power of growth. It must not only have roots, but it must be free to rise and expand out of the dark earth in which it has been protected and encased, into the universal sunshine and air. It must not fear to crumble into dust, like some dead thing at a touch from outside. On the contrary, it must be exposed to all the winds of heaven and the tempests that shake the earth, all adverse and benign influence, using all for purposes and material of growth, steadily rising and spreading always, reaching out mighty, outstretching arms and generous branch after branch, where all men may come and find shelter and repose. Let us not be deceived. The Jewish idea survives, but only on condition that it shall not so expand, that it shall not rise into freedom and light; only on condition that it shall remain fixed and stationary, prolonging its existence by artificial and external means, rather than by process of inner and organic growth.

And what, then, is this Jewish ideal for which we must live or die, in contradistinction to the Christian ideal?

The Jewish ideal, we are told by those who would draw the distinction, is justice. The Christian ideal is love. The Jewish ideal places the emphasis on the life, the practice, the Law fulfilled as law, as duty, as morality enforced from on high. "Thus saith the Lord." The Christian places it on faith, on the Law fulfilled as love, which gives the impulse, the motive, and the power whereby to fulfil the Law, and therefore the *life* of the moral deed.

Is there then radical opposition and antagonism between the two? Does the one exclude the other? I think it does, unless we are willing to believe that the greater includes the less, the whole in-

cludes the part, reconciles and completes
it. Only through love is the true moral
life attained, the moral law fulfilled, explained, and justified, touched and quickened into a passionate holiness, instead
of a soulless code of external obligation
and conformity. Love *is* religion, the
binding force of the universe, — that
which binds man close to man, which
binds man close to God. Only to the
eye of love that pierces the very heart
of things and searches the inward part
and reins, can justice ever be revealed.

And this then is the crucial test, the
kernel of difference. We may do away
with rabbinism, we may strip away husk
after husk of outward distinction, all
artificial barriers and enactments of separation, every badge and label that di-
vides the Jew from the rest of the world;
but here, and here alone, hidden in the
depths of the spiritual life, is the truth

that shall set us free and make us one with our fellows, because it makes all men truly brothers, children of one loving Father, and all alike sharers of the divine life. " For there is no difference between the Jew and the Greek; for the same Lord over all is rich unto those who call upon Him."

How little the world has yet realised or even understood this ideal, how far removed is the kingdom of peace on earth and good-will to men, no people better than the Jews can testify, — " in stripes and in imprisonments, in wanderings by land and sea, in cold and darkness, hunger and thirst, patience and long-suffering." For that very reason are we, the Jews, above all others, the ones to hasten its coming, to give our life, our soul, to further, not to hinder it ; to make it a reality, not a mockery, an actuality as well as an ideal. Then, and then only, "will death be swallowed up in victory; and the Lord God will wipe away tears from off all faces; and the rebuke of His people shall He take away from off all the earth: for the Lord hath spoken it."

"But we are born," you say, "into a race and religion." Yes, but we must be born again into larger and higher conditions than this race and this religion permit, into more spiritual relations, not only with our fellow-beings, but with God; into a more vitalised and liberating faith. We must be born again, not of the flesh, but of the spirit, which apprehends God, which recognises and reveals Him in close and tender relation, personally and individually, to each and all of us. And this is the Messiah, the Counsellor and inward messenger that brings peace to the soul, — not *a* man, *a* God, but the spirit that abides with all men and makes God manifest according to our capacity to receive and apprehend Him. Whether or not this spirit has ever incarnated itself in its human and ideal perfection in any being that has walked the earth, any actual or historic personage, or whether it will ever so incarnate itself, is the point where Jews and Christians divide.

But whatever theology may have done to distort and pervert, whatever modification and foreign admixture may have crept in, in passing through so many minds, so many families and races of men, the Messianic idea is no less essential to Judaism than to Christianity. Without it Judaism is maimed, imperfect, and can never hope to carry salvation to the Gentiles and publish peace to all the world. We hear little of it now among the Jews; but we cannot let it go as we have done from our spiritual consciousness without spiritual loss. We cannot let it lapse, as we have done, or be lost in some vague millennial dream of temporal welfare and prosperity; for it has grown to be a personal gift and possession of mankind, a psychological fact, a vital necessity of man's inmost being. Once having conceived this ultimate redemption, nothing short of a divinely-perfected humanity can content us, — man rising to God, God stooping to man, the human and divine so merged that each is recognised in and of the other, a spiritual presence everywhere. There is no idolatry in this when rightly understood. On the contrary, it does away with idolatry; for it places no concrete image, no visible form, between God and His creatures, but draws each man in his own spirit, in his own likeness, up to God, according as God has fashioned him.

The work of the intellect is singular.

Men have intuitively apprehended the
great spiritual truths. Then comes the
intellect, weighing and measuring and
casting everything into its own mould,
shaping and adapting the truths of God
to suit men's limited comprehension; and
so we have dogma, hard and unyielding,
almost quenching the spirit and the
truth. Then when the intellect has out-
grown its own limitations, and when the
world is ready for a purer form of the
spirit, a clearer expression of the truth,
this self-same intellect turns and rends
what it had created, destroys what it
had so elaborately built up. But the
spirit shines out undimmed, more luminous than ever. Thus the idea of God
has undergone many idolatrous phases.
The idea of the Messiah must pass
through the same process of purification
and evolution.

The problem of Judaism is more diffi-

cult than that of any other religion. We
are constantly being recruited, as it were,
from below. The tide of immigration
pours into us its troubled waters, — the
ignorant, the superstitious, the outcast,
the outlandish of the nations, the slaves of
centuries of bondage. To feed, to clothe,
to shelter them, to give them bodily com-
forts, is a task taxing our utmost strength.
To feed them spiritually is a task almost
beyond our strength. For a while they
may be satisfied to practise their religion,
to shut themselves off from other men;
but who can doubt that, breathing the
air of freedom, scenting the battle from
afar, like so many others, they will cast
off the chains that oppress them and
fling themselves into the fray, the mad
rush and struggle for material things that
leaves neither time nor room for other
pre-occupations? Says Mr. Zangwill, —

"Russia and America are the two

strongholds of the race, and Russia is
pouring her streams into America, where
they will be made free men and free
thinkers. It is in America, then, that
the last great battle of Judaism will be
fought out; amid the temples of the
New World it will make its last struggle
to survive."

The strength of the Jewish life lies, I
am told, "in the great body of sound,
normal, commonplace lives which go to
make up the strength or the weakness (?)
of the life of every community." But
let us look a little more closely into this
same body of "normal, commonplace
lives." Shall we not find here, as elsewhere, a lurking discontent, a sense of
personal grievance and disadvantage, and
at the same time a galled and sensitive
pride that chafes under their Judaism?
And, one hardly dares whisper it, shall
we not also find even here anti-Semi-

tism cropping out against any class less
qualified, less modernised than their
own ?

But even if such a sound body of
commonplace lives existed, I do not think
they would fitly represent Judaism, unless Judaism is content to remain a commonplace and insignificant element in
modern civilisation.   On the contrary,
I think there will only be strength in
Israel when there shall arise great leaders, lifted above just this sordid common-
placeness, this official and banded Phil-
istinism; men of daring thought and
action, in touch with their people through
sympathy and appreciation, but in touch
also with the larger spiritual and religious movement of their times; men
who feel acutely the need, and the heavy
weight of their responsibility, — who are
not afraid to pluck religion out of the
temples and synagogues where it has

slumbered, out of the dead forms and
effete rites, and carry it into the heart
of life, to set free the God so long imprisoned in the ark of the covenant, and
make Him a living presence in the
world ; men who have renounced the
visible temporal church in order to
enter the Church Universal, the church
invisible that is not of time or space,
where the saints and seers of all time,
the " illumined " of all sects, all creeds,
and all races have ever worshipped and
will worship through the ages.

They only are the saviours of the people
who, recognising the tremendous significance of the past, recognise also the tremendous significance of the present ; who
are alive and awake to the call, the
message of the hour, ready for joyful
sacrifice and fulfilment, knowing the
time has come when Israel shall take
her place among the nations, her war-

fare accomplished, triumphant, crowned with the spiritual crown of sacrifice, the sign and promise of a kingdom that is not of the earth.

May, 1894.

THE TASK OF JUDAISM.

LONG ago has our nineteenth century been branded as an age of unbelief and materialism, of vanished faith and ideals, of religious indifference or positive revolt. In reality it has been a period of intense religious ferment and upheaval, of moral and spiritual conflict, of religious growth and evolution. It has been a time to try men's souls, to test and strain to the utmost the faith that was in them; for it has seemed that the powers of light as well as of darkness, the dictates of reason, of science, and of conscience, conspired to force man to surrender, to deny his highest right and privilege, to make him the tool, the victim of blind chance or blind necessity, of laws so fixed and inexorable as forever to chain him to matter and hopelessly bind the wings of his spirit. Happily that time has passed, or is passing ; and there is no more significant fact than the changed attitude of the world's thought to-day on these great topics. Like the light slowly creeping over the mountain tops, God is coming back into His world.   His name appears again where it had been banished.   Men are no longer afraid of that highest conception of their intellect and heart, that supreme postulate of their reason, the sole cause and end of their being.

But it is a changed conception that they hold, and one that no longer fits in with the old theologies, the established creeds and worship, the limitations of doctrine and sect.   Within the churches to some extent, but still more outside of the churches, a new current has set in, — a breaking free from dogma and prescribed form; a broadening and expansion of the religious life that shows a new force at work, — a force that men had tried to imprison within fixed and narrow articles of faith (so-called), but that can no more be imprisoned than the wind can be imprisoned, " which bloweth, like the spirit, where it listeth." It is not that a new religion has come into the world, but that religion is being born from a lower to a higher plane, — out of the realm of material forms, the systems men have built around it, the body with which it has been clothed, into the realm of spirit, a purely inner kingdom, where alone man meets God, and God meets man. According to the freedom with which any religion expands to this ideal, without losing its content and identity; according to the richness and the fulness of the spiritual life, the closeness of union and communion so attained,—will be the measure and the scope of that religion as a factor and a working-power in the world's spiritual progress. To this tribunal now comes every sect of Christendom and every form of Judaism.

We Jews are apt to think that we are not broken up into sects like other religions; that, in spite of external and intellectual difference, a Jew is a Jew the world over, bound by some ineradicable bond that no force of circumstance or environment has the power or the right to break. In reality, we are broken up into almost as many sects as units. Each man is a law unto himself,— that is to say, he is an expounder and interpreter of the law according to his own wisdom. The division of "orthodox" and "reform" suffices to cover the whole range of Judaism, the whole field of religious activity and debate, embracing opinions the most diverse and contradictory, and types the most opposite that can be conceived. At one extreme we have mediævalism, the still unburied ghost, wrapped round with all the mummery of the past, — dead form, dead rites, dead letter, — that haunts the Ghetto and bids us beware how we step beyond those sacred walls. At the other extreme we have nineteenth century progress and reform, the liberal and enlightened rabbi, who tells us, —

"Assuredly, if you will, we are ready to give up our peculiar traits and customs, if these offend; to abolish religious or ceremonial rites which the spirit of the age cannot approve; to abandon fringes and phylacteries. Nay, more, indeed, we have already done so, and have consigned them to the lumber-room of the past, in order to make room for the decrees of modern æstheticism."

And this accomplished, let me ask, What have you given in their place? What have you now to give that will take the place of so much that was vital and integral to the faith as your fathers and forefathers conceived it, and as many still conceive it, — the vast system of rules and regulations that has been so laboriously and so conscientiously built up, on which all the spiritual energies, the practical piety and devotion of your people, have been expended for untold generations; the method of their holiness, by which, however crudely, they brought God into their lives, in personal, concrete, and direct relation, — the very life of Judaism in the sense that it permeates the whole scheme and process of daily living? To take all this away, to set all this aside, and put nothing in its place, is to leave a gap which the ordinary mind, the average religious consciousness of

men, cannot possibly supply. What have
you now to give, what have you now to
teach, to offset the world's teachings and
the world's gifts ?

Look around you. See the defection
everywhere, the indifference, the neglect
and lack of interest in things spiritual and
religious, the widespread and ever-growing unbelief and secularism. From all
sides sounds a cry of warning and alarm.
In Germany, we are told, "ninety-five per
cent of the Jewish youth is *atheistic*, and
at best utterly *indifferent*. The other five
per cent are *divided* between orthodoxy
and reform." In England, says a reverend
doctor, " it is a critical time for Judaism.
The synagogues become less and less fre-
quented. In vain they are made splendid
and luxurious; in vain the organ lends
its solemn, awe-inspiring strains, — . . .
the synagogues are less and less fre-
quented." Says another authority, "Our

people are spiritually starved ; " and from
Jewish mothers comes the plaint, —

"What shall we teach our children?
Is there any reason why we should grow
up and raise our little ones without religion? . . . For we are raising them
without religion. I repeat, we are raising
up, here in our midst, and in the midst
of other congregations, a generation without religion. Oh, yes, we have our Sun-
day-schools. You send your children
there, but for what? To learn ancient
history and the rudiments of a dead
language. Do you call *that* religion?
. . . Religion means far more than the
repetition of a series of kings or judges,
or a list of tribes, with perhaps the abil-
ity stumblingly to read through a given
number of Hebrew prayers with their
translations. . . . All the knowledge of
an ancient history and of a dead language will never hold one child loyal

to the faith of his fathers. . . . Whose
the fault, and where does the responsibility lie? It matters not. . . . But
rather what is the remedy?"

And from opposite camps we hear the
old, old cry, — "Orthodoxy" on the one
side, and on the other "Reform;" neither
seeing the pitfalls of the other, neither
seeing that it is just on these rocks that
we have split and gone to pieces. The
props have been removed, the strongholds
deserted, that had long been guarded at
such fearful cost; and Judaism has been
left defenceless to battle with the world
alone, and open to the enemy.

"Nay, not so fast," you will protest;
"Judaism does not stand, does not fall,
with orthodoxy or reform. Judaism *is*
founded on a rock, — the rock of the
moral law, firm as the foundations of
the earth, that cannot be moved. All
else may pass, all forms, all shows, but

this remains. Judaism in its essence is so simple, so sublime a thing: not a complex ecclesiasticism, not a doctrinal or dogmatic creed, not a theory or abstract speculation, but a religion of life, the moral life itself, the moral law ordained by God, — 'To do justice, to love mercy, and to walk humbly with thy God.' "

A simple code, no doubt; and yet how does it come that throughout our history, in tragic and in prosperous times, in order to bring it even dimly to the apprehension of our people, to make it valid as a working principle, — "a religion of life," as you say, — it has always been found necessary to supplement it with the ceremonial code, which, with all its intricacy and its ramifications, has been more easily and more lovingly followed? In vain did the Prophets exhort and denounce: in their

days, as in ours, we have always been
able and willing to bring our sacrifice
and burnt-offering. The sacrifice of the
heart we have not yet learned how to
bring. The Law, even in its most literal,
most technical shape, has been our con-
solation and delight; upon it have we
meditated day and night. And not without reason, for it has had its roots deep
down in the very constitution of our
Judaism; it has been our link and medi-
ator with the divine, our religion, inasmuch as it bound us to one another and
bound us to God at the same time that
it effectually separated us from the rest
of mankind. Can we wonder, then, that
this being withdrawn, the Law having
lost its hold and stringency, its unifying
and sanctifying power, the people should
scatter and fall apart, should waver and
grow confused in their allegiance, and
that the house should be divided against
itself ?

And the cause of this does not lie merely in the removal of outward restraint and compulsion, but still more in the lack of inward compulsion and harmony, the need of an inner motive and incentive that should give sanctity and consecration to life. Not merely that we should set aside intellectual difference, and unite among ourselves upon some common ground, some point of law or doctrine, some common rule of life even, but that in the very heart of life there should be unity and peace. And for this we must look deeper than the ceremonial, deeper even than the moral law, — in which it was never intended that we should find ultimate rest, because it is not the end of our being, the fulfilment and satisfaction of our spiritual nature, the rock on which we can finally repose.

The mistake we make lies in pinning our faith to any law, even the most sub-

lime. The Law has been our strength,
— it has also been our stumbling-
block, our fetich and graven image at
times. In it we have put all our trust.
"It is not God's truth, it is not God's
law, — it is God that is the salvation
of the world." The moral law may
be a more spiritual rendering than the
ceremonial of our relation to God; but it
does not give us the whole truth of that
relation, the last word of holiness, which
means oneness with the Divine, any more
than it gives us the whole content of
our human relations. The moral law
does not of necessity lead us to God,
although it may lead us to the heights
of human and heroic endeavour : whether
it also lead us " beyond," into conscious
relation with something or some one that
is above and beyond the human, is largely
a matter of our own special needs and
temperament.

The essence of a faith, then, lies not alone in its moral efficacy, but in the spirit and freedom of its obedience, and its free access to God; in the instant recognition of a divine impulse, a divine Presence in the soul, which the moral law does not necessarily evoke, but from which the moral law necessarily flows as a loving trust and obedience. "Climb the moral heights within," you say, "rise to the moral truth, and thou too shalt receive from God the tablets of His law." Nay, but rather let it be "according to your faith," — that is, according to your inward vision, your sense of this Presence, your power to discern the hidden truth, the deepest meaning of life, the eternal reality beneath the appearance, which we call God; above all, according to your power to trust this vision of God in your life, and in all life, through whatever cloud, whatever hindrance of temperament or circumstance, will be the measure of your strength to rise and reach those shining heights.

Religion does not begin and end with the moral law, but includes it in its larger, deeper scope. " Though I were perfect, yet would I not know my own soul," says Job. Religion, in its fullest sense — namely, service, loving service to God and man — is not satisfied with justice and with duty, grand and commanding though these ideals may be. " There is a word over all, beautiful as the sky," falling like the rain and the sunshine on the just and the unjust. We may climb the moral heights perforce, we may tread the lofty summits of duty ; " we may do justice and love mercy ;" " we may bestow our goods to feed the poor, and give our body to be burned, — but if we have not charity [a love and insight rather divine than human] it profiteth nothing."

"But society cannot be founded on love," says the exponent of Judaism, who insists "that it is just here where Christianity errs, and proves itself so inferior to Judaism, so inadequate in its conception and scheme of life, — a religion for children and undeveloped nations, not for mature and thinking men." "Justice," he tells us, "is definite, and love indefinite. Justice each can claim from each and all; love none can claim from any. That which justice bids be done is predicable and verifiable as a mathematical problem; justice is indeed a form of applied mathematics. That which love bids be done is not predicable and is not verifiable, it is always an unknown quantity. It is quite obvious, therefore, that justice can and that love cannot furnish a basis for legislation, for the regulation of human affairs."

Apart from the astounding claim that

justice is or could ever be made an exact science, "a form of applied mathematics," — could ever be so accurately weighed and measured in the human understanding as to furnish an infallible basis, an infallible standard and guide for human affairs, — how is it possible to conceive of a living, breathing human society, a group of erring, aspiring human beings, as a mathematical problem, a group of mathematical units requiring mathematical test and treatment? If such were the perfect society, then better the most imperfect that has yet been evolved.

But without stopping to consider so extraordinary a statement, I would only call to mind a simple fact. The root of society is the family. Is the family founded on justice, — or, in this case, does not justice freely flow from love? And is the family therefore less stable, or rather more so, than society, because its basis is more organic, more deeply rooted in the very constitution of things? The primitive man, the savage, recognises no tie beyond self, — no larger relation, no love but self-love. Out of this evolves family love, with its sacred ties, its tender and holy association. Out of this evolves the State, with its complex relations, its almost infinite promise and scope. Far, far distant are we yet from this larger ideal of human progress and growth, — of love, or even of justice, in this largest of human relations. And yet justice belongs to the more rudimentary plane and type of society. It is the preparation for love, — the claim that *can* be enforced, prior to the claim that does not *need* to be enforced. Justice is not done away with by love, but is simply deepened and enriched, — taking deeper root, lifting itself into higher and more aspiring growth.

Finally, in regard to our relation with a Supreme Being, the same critic tells us : "From man to God there can be love, and this love is the very essence of religion ; but from God to man there cannot be love, because love expresses a human emotion, having in it an element of yearning and a desire for possession, — and to ascribe love to God is an anthropopathism, just as the ascription to God of hands or eyes is an anthropomorphism."

And in the first place, it seems to me that even in its human aspect love has something more of the divine than is here attributed to it. But setting this aside, if there cannot be love from God to man, still less can there be justice on either side. "How should a man be just with God ?" and "In God's sight can no man living be justified." Moreover, a God with a conscience, a moral sense, is as "anthro-

popathic" as a God with a heart or an
emotional sense.   The moral is no less a
purely human attribute and measurement.
Whatever we know or predicate of God
transcends our moralities just as much as
it transcends our emotions, — even as the
heavens are high above the earth.

But even that dread word, anthropomorphism, has lost some of its terrors
these last few years.   Even scientists are
beginning to acknowledge that a God of
humanity must have something in common with humanity ; otherwise *we* could
not love Him.   And this love " is the
very essence of religion," you say.   Surely
God were less, not more, than human if
He could not love us, His children, whom
He has created in His own image and
likeness, whom He pities even as a father
pities his children.   And I think we
should often find in the life and religious
experience of many people that this love

— or rather the awakening into it, the growing knowledge and consciousness of it — had been the very beginning of the spiritual life, the leading out from darkness into light. " Say to your friend, your child, 'God loves you;' say it in every language of yours, in every vernacular of his, which you can command." So teaches Phillips Brooks, and I think there is inspiration in the words.

But these are themes that do not admit of argument or proof on any side, and must rather come before the judgment seat of each individual soul. Let us return then to the main point, the living, practical issue. Our people are crying for bread and we are giving them a stone.

I wish to point out the fact that there are two aspects of the problem before us, the crisis we have come upon, — the one in our outer, external life, in our unsolved

and unsatisfactory relations with the
people around us; the other and far
deeper one, it seems to me, in ourselves,
in our inner life, in those deeper principles and convictions in which we had
thought ourselves forever grounded and
fixed. And I cannot help feeling that
the solution of the one depends primarily
upon the other; the solution of both depends primarily upon ourselves. From
within as well as from without we are
confronted with new conditions, grave
needs which we seem in no wise prepared to meet: from within rather than
from without must come the answers,
the guiding light to a new and larger
destiny. Whatever may have been true
of the past, the key of the situation lies
now in our hands.

But it cannot be by the old methods
and formulæ, the old stereotyped answers,
that we can hope to unravel it. Both

"orthodoxy" and "reform" have alike proved their inadequacy. The new wine cannot be put into old bottles, else the bottles break. Still more foolhardy and presumptuous were it, however, to attempt to give a panacea for all the ills our people are heir to; to find an instant and definite solution, a complete settlement, of all our doubts and difficulties that should at once cover all the facts and appeal to all intelligences. There can only be gradual growth and emancipation according to our lights, our opportunities, and understanding; gradual adjustment and adaptation to our new environment, whether temporal or spiritual, — a long, difficult, and laborious process. But it must be a growth from within of greater freedom and light, not a gift from without.

And if ever in the distant future we can hope to see the so-called Jewish ques-

tion settled, it is we ourselves, and not
the people around us, who must settle it.
It is we ourselves who must lay it at rest
by living in larger questions than those
of race or sect or narrow creed, in larger
religious sympathies and toleration, in the
larger *spirit* of our faith in a universal
Father, rather than in the restrictions
and bondage of the letter that would con-
fine it exclusively to our peculiar Jewish
dispensation. In a word, it must be a
change of heart and spirit, of inner motive and attitude, rather than of circumstance. Circumstances have changed and
are changing all the time around us, and
yet, in a sense, *we* do not change. The
Jew remains the Jew, separated by alien
traditions, by almost invincible antago-
nisms, from the people with whom he
dwells in close daily living and contact.
However much, however little we base it
on, whether as race or religion, the primal

fact with us remains our Judaism, our
survival as Jews, distinct from the people
around us, — a survival, a distinction
always to be insisted upon, not as a
large, all-embracing spiritual idea and
fellowship that welcomes other expression of the truth besides its own, but,
on the contrary, as a principle that under
some form, some pretext or another,
always isolates and excludes.

It were idle to attribute solely to
others, and therefore to resent with such
bitter heart-burning, that very aloofness
which is the basis of our own existence.
It is we who draw the lines and make
the terms and conditions, who call out
to the people around us: " Thus far and
no farther ! We will buy with you, we
will sell with you, we will give and take ;
but bone of our bone, flesh of our flesh,
spirit of our spirit, shall you not be.
For we are a holy and consecrated race,

unto whom, and unto whom alone, God's truth has been conveyed in order that we may hand it down intact to our children and our children's children after them."

A logical position, if you will; but then we must abide by it, and be willing to take the consequences. We must be content with our isolation and exclusion, our little corner of Palestine, our Jerusalem old or new, the Ghettos of our own making. We must remain Hebrews among Hebrews, a peculiar race, a peculiar sect, whose very existence betokens separation, whose only claim can be for recognition *as such* a sect and race, — for *toleration,* not for perfectly free and equal acceptance by people of alien birth and belief. Presupposing narrowness, we naturally find narrowness; we invite it and we meet it again and again, generally of a more malignant type than our

own, in others more ignorant than ourselves, or more endowed with social and
worldly advantage. But we can hardly
expect that even the most well-disposed
of those outside our faith should not
make their own reservations and exclu-
sions, and draw their own conclusions.
We can hardly expect that they should
regard as universal a religion that requires so many safeguards and precau-
tions in order to secure its continuance,
or that the world should be edified by
ideals that necessarily move in so small
a compass.

"Not ours the fault!" you exclaim.
"The Jew is ready. The Jew hopes and
prays for the time when his religion as
distinguished from others shall no longer
be. The Jew is ready, and has been for
some time, to plunge into the ocean of humanity. But the world is not ready; the
time is not ripe. The ocean of humanity

does not as yet invite us to its invigorating waves. The poisoned arrows of hate are still abroad, still seeking the Jew as a target. The fault is not ours. The Jew cannot say when the time shall be for him to disappear. The world at large has to fix the hour."

And it is just exactly here where you are wrong. It *is* for the Jew to sound the note of his own freedom, when he is ready for it, to *claim* it, rather than wait for the world to fix the hour, for the world to give it to him. It is for the Jew himself to throw off the chains that bind him, whether of his own or the world's making; to break down the barriers, the walls of defiance or defence, behind which he has so long been forced to shelter himself; and to stand free among free men, "with the glorious liberty of the sons of God, of those who are led by the spirit of God, and for whom the whole creation waits." If the Jew is ready for this and does not do it, then his own words condemn him. The world cannot hinder, the world cannot bring it about. And, in the face of anti-Semitism, I believe that the world will recognise it when the Jew actually is free. Anti-Semitism cannot make, cannot keep us Jews, any more than it can make Christians of us, if we have no better reason for being either the one or the other. That were a low view of Judaism. Like a dark cloud upon the horizon, anti-Semitism still lingers in lands where darkness lingers. In America, in such shadowy form as it appears, it disappears again like a cloud when we ignore it, when we have learned to live far and away above and beyond it, in the peace and freedom of large and liberated ideas. We bear a charmed life; the slings and arrows of hate pass us by unharmed, because they no longer touch us. We

11

are not traitors, we are not cowards who desert our less fortunate brethren, the oppressed and persecuted of our race. On the contrary, "if we would lift them, we must stand on higher ground than they," and the best and most loyal service we can do them, is to lead them gently but firmly where they too may be finally beyond the range of persecution and hate. Here in America we stand on such a vantage ground, we survey so wide a field, — the whole stretch of our civilisation as it were, conditions so various, opportunities so vast, — that here if anywhere the problem must resolve itself. By almost imperceptible and insensible gradations, the East seems to merge and be lost in the West, the old seems to melt in the new, and Israel to disappear in the vast ocean of humanity.

Like the gathering of the waters they come on every side, — from the dark ages

one might almost say, the benighted lands
where no ray of freedom has ever reached.
We do not say to these bewildered and
belated wanderers from other climes and
times: "Keep your jargon and your uncouth ways and customs. Insist upon
being Russians, Poles, Roumanians, for
on no account must you lose your nationality and identity." On the contrary, we
bid them welcome only on condition that
they *shall* lose it, that they shall become
Americans as we are ; we teach them what
it means to be free, and in a generation
their children are free-born Americans.
And so too with our Jewish nationality.
We cannot expect to become citizens of
the world while we remain citizens of
Judæa, bound by local ties, local prejudice and interests; so long as we insist
upon perpetuating a race-tie that separates us from the people around us.

But there is still a deeper question involved, which in reality includes the other two. Politically, socially, we may be free, or we may become so in time through the gradual process of emancipation and amalgamation, conditioned to a certain degree, upon the political and social status of the nation among whom we happen to dwell. But there is another freedom into which we can only enter through our own initiative, our own effort or aspiration, and at such time and in such degree as we may be ready for it. Few of us may suspect, perhaps, and still fewer be willing to acknowledge, the lack among us of spiritual and religious freedom, — of that freedom of the soul, of the spirit "which bloweth where it listeth," and which leaves us free to go forth beyond our own borders, to seek, to find, to share the spiritual life, wherever and however it may meet us.

Pent up so long in our Jewries, we do

not realise how exclusive, how concentrated, how intensely Jewish our thought, our whole point of view has become. Whoever has transcended it has of necessity been ostracised. Witness Spinoza, Maimonides even, " who is cursed as a heretic and perverter of the Law." We do not realise how completely we have been shut out from the larger spiritual life of the world around us, from all spiritual contact and intercourse with any but our little band of so-called co-religionists; how limited in consequence are our sympathies in this direction, and how hampered our judgment. We may know somewhat of the history of the Christian *Church,* its errors, its follies, and its crimes, especially in dealing with ourselves; we may know somewhat of Christian *Doctrine,* the teachings and opinions of men; but of that inner life of the world whose course and whose shaping are due to Christian thought and influence, — that is to say, to the life and spirit of Christ, — we know very little, nor are we willing to acquiesce in what little we do know. We are still largely under the impression that religiously, as compared with ourselves, the nations around us are sunk in darkness.

However liberal-minded we may hold ourselves to be, however emancipated, however indifferent to the forms of our own faith, our glory and our pride still lie in the fact that we are *not* Christians, but outside of the pale as much as ever, and as firmly persuaded that no good can come out of Nazareth. In our heart of hearts we know very well that not for an instant do we tolerate Christianity, or look upon it other than as an aberration, a perversion of Judaism, " a degrading form of error," of superstition, of idolatry and man-worship. The very name of Christ is a sacrilege in our eyes, a standing menace and reproach, a violation of our sacred principle of monotheism, at which our Jewish sensibilities spring to arms or shrink within themselves, chilled and repelled. But why should we, and we alone, be conscious of this moral shock, when even within doctrinal limits we see how wide a field, how large a latitude, is possible, — as evidenced by the number and diversity of Christian sects, ranging from High-Church Episcopalian to Unitarianism; above all, when we remember how commanding a place this conception in some form or other, this personality, has taken in the civilisation of which we form a part, in the almost universal religious consciousness of men among whom we desire to dwell?

We think others narrow, or less enlightened than ourselves, who are not

willing or able to receive our doctrine,
our version of the truth, our conception
of the Deity, our ideas of the world's
moral and social regeneration; and yet
whatever we may do in secular matters,
in religious and spiritual matters we do
not allow a ray of light to penetrate
from outside. We do not even conceive
or acknowledge that there can be any
light, any vision but our own, — so firmly
have we believed what our fathers have
told us from the beginning; so confident,
so secure are we that the truth we hold
about God is all the truth that men
have ever known, all that they can ever
know, all they need to know, and that
therefore our mission consists in guarding this truth unsullied from the world
until the world is worthy to receive it.

The question I would ask now is: Are
we justified in this belief; and does the
spiritual condition of our people bear

witness to it, either to the people around us or among ourselves? Where are our spiritual teachers? What are our contributions to the spiritual thought of the world? Open our "religious" books, our Jewish magazines and periodicals, — what shall we find but arid, technical, legal discussion — exegetical treatises, learned disquisitions perhaps, on some obscure point of law or doctrine, the root of some Hebrew word, the source of some far-away tradition, — purely sectarian questions, that could only concern us as a narrow local sect, and could have no universal significance or application, no possible relation, to the world at large, — Jewish topics for a Jewish audience?

Is this all that we can lay claim to, all that we can aspire to, — we, who hold God's truth in the hollow of our hand? Not a breath of the spirit anywhere, not a hint of the spiritual life truly so-called.

Cramped within our narrow borders, we are stifled for lack of air to breathe, for lack of room to grow, for lack of life, spiritual life, — the life which is more than food or raiment, more than deeds or creeds, which comes down to us from above, and is the free gift of God to those who are free to receive and therefore free to give.

It is not enough, as we have seen, to lop off excrescences, to rub away the dust and mould of centuries, the Ghetto accumulation of effete rites and customs, so long as our spirit is not free to rise above Jewish horizons and boundary lines, to see that in God's boundless universe all truth, all spirit are one, alike for the Jew and the Christian who live in the spirit and the truth. It is not enough to humanise, to liberalise, to " moralise," or secularise our religion. What we need is to spiritualise it by making our relation

with God, and thence our relation with
men, a more vital and therefore a more
spiritual one than can be based on law in
any form. Law is of the natural order,
and love is of the spiritual order; hence
law can never be the fundamental relation which binds us to one another as
spiritual beings, and to God as spirit.
Law can only be the tutelage through
which we must pass to higher freedom, —
that freedom of the spirit which is life,
spiritual life, because it lives in the spirit,
not the letter of man's obedience, in the
motive rather than the deed, and which
is therefore love in the highest, — "the
unknown quantity," if you will, because it
puts that touch of the Infinite into life
and gives the *beauty* of holiness, "the
light that never was on sea or land," and
yet "the master-light of all our seeing;"
which cannot be predicated, which cannot be verified, because it transcends hu-

man logic and proof; which cannot be bound, which cannot be claimed nor conditioned, but must always remain a free gift, freely given and freely received, — the perfect love which casts out fear, " the peace which passes understanding."

Is this Christianity? Is it Judaism? What does it matter? Side by side, shoulder to shoulder, stand the Christian and the Jew, their task precisely the same, their destiny strangely bound together; no longer separated even by arbitrary and external distinctions, still less by any *real* distinction, and yet divided as ever in heart and spirit and allegiance, unable or unwilling to recognise each other as brothers in the deepest sense, children of the same spiritual Father, heirs of the true faith which by its largeness, its power to satisfy the deepest spiritual needs of men, shall overcome the world.

One of the most spiritually-minded of

our New England women, whose life and
letters have just been published, writes
thus to a Jew : " I have always had the
idea that Jew and Christian were really
one ; only they did not understand each
other." And, again, Claude Montefiore
in a recent article says : " The doctrine
of Jesus may be regarded as pure Christianity or pure Judaism. Either way
contains a truth." Whence comes, then,
this tragic misunderstanding, this gulf of
separation that the ages have not been
able to bridge over?

"I come not to send peace on earth,
but a sword." The words ring down
through the centuries. It is Christ the
Jew, Christ the Christian, who has set
at variance the Christian with the Jew,
"the parent with the child, the brother
with the brother." Nor will the sword
be laid aside until Christian and Jew
alike, until all mankind, come to a better

understanding of the truth of love he taught, the life of love he lived, the way of love he showed, by which all men, without respect of persons or condition — not alone the prophet and the saint, the holy men of Israel, the elect of the world, but the sinner and the outcast and the lost sheep, the least of His little ones — should come nigh the Father.

"Ah, but," you exclaim, "for well-nigh two thousand years this religion of love has been taught, has been preached from how many pulpits, in how many lands, and what has come of it? Corruption in high places and in low; a society built on selfishness, whose very pillars are greed; a ruinous competition which drives the weak ones to the wall, and poverty stalking grim and gaunt among us, unloving and unloved. Church after church rears its heaven-pointed spire, its golden cross, aloft among the

dwellings of the rich, while the poor live
huddled together in wretched tenements
not fit for dumb beasts of burden. Here
in our own city a leading church has
just openly avowed itself a 'moneyed
corporation' whose first interest was
'business' interest, pledged to secure
the greatest amount of revenue possible
for the building of its churches and the
spread of its faith. Said a labour leader
who recently visited New York, 'You
have too many churches here,' for it is
churches such as these that widen the
breach between the rich and the poor,
that make the irreligion, not the religion
of the masses. If this be the religion of
love, we will have none of it. Let the
Christian better live up to his ideal;
let him give the example, and perhaps
we will follow; let him prove by his
deeds of charity and love the superiority
of his faith over ours, and then, mayhap,

we will be convinced, — or rather, no,
we shall not need to be convinced, for
his faith will then be as ours. When
men have ceased to persecute and hate,
then justice will be established upon the
earth, and all men will be brothers."

But, no, I say unto you, not so. It
is we who may give the example; we
who may lead, not wait to follow. It is
we who may teach the religion of love
as it has never yet been taught, who
may practise and spread it, — we who
have proved ourselves capable of living
and of dying for an ideal. Here is our
great mission, our opportunity as a spiritual people scattered among the nations,
in whose breast smoulders the sacred
fire, in whose veins courses the blood of
prophet and of priest. Shall we be
content with petty points of law, with
paltry measuring of anise and cummin,
and, gathering our skirts of holiness

about us, go our way undefiled, in conscious pride of rectitude? Has God no
larger purpose, no higher destiny in store
for us, His chosen people whom He has
so miraculously preserved, whom He has
led through the wilderness into the
promised land, out of captivity into
freedom? No longer let it be, to the
nations around us: "Stand back, for ye
are less holy than we are," but rather
once again as before, from one of our
race: "Come unto me, for I am meek
and lowly of heart. Come learn of me,
for I will teach you to know God, — not
in pillar of cloud and fire, in awful might
and majesty, but in gentle ministry of
love, as from father to son, from parent
to little child, from loving friend to friend.
I will make incarnate in myself this
power and will to love, and thus reveal
the Father to His children in loving
unity of spirit and likeness, — the human

12

even as one with the divine. And for this I offer myself — in sacrifice? No; but rather in consummation, in consecration, of the whole life, the whole being, to do the Father's will and so make known His doctrine."

"The world is not ready," you say? In a sense, the world is never ready; and yet the truth comes to be known, the truth must be taught, though its teachers die in the teaching. But I believe that the world is waiting even now for this truth to be put into life, for this heavenly message of love, for the messenger that comes in the name of the Lord, that brings good tidings of good, that publisheth peace and salvation, — peace on earth to all men of God's will. For the world has awakened to its needs. The thousand schemes for social reform prove that many a man is ready and willing to sell all he has and give to the poor, if only he knew

how best to help his neighbour. But the
Church is not ready; the Church is not
willing to give up anything to which it
clings, of the goods of this world or another, its temporal or its spiritual power,
— and so the Church has lost its influence, for men see the hollowness of its
claim. The world is no longer deceived
by false gods and false doctrines, by a
false worship of Mammon that calls itself Christianity. Nor yet will it turn
to a Judaism stamped with narrowness.
Not even the Judaism which the Prophets
preached, but that which they prophesied,
when "sorrow and sighing shall flee
away," and "the earth shall be filled
with the knowledge of the Lord as the
waters cover the sea," is that which shall
unite the Jewish and the Christian ideal;
and what God has thus joined together
in deepest spiritual union, let no man
keep asunder.

But, practically, what shall we do?
I am asked indignantly: "Shall we
abandon Judaism? If so, what are we
to substitute for it? Shall we join the
ranks of the atheists, or seek refuge in
the dominant Church? There is no
other alternative. And, if not, then
where shall we find our fellowship under
existing conditions? . . . To give up Judaism now, to merge with the world at
large spiritually at this time would be
an act of wanton self-destruction, a sacri-
rifice great and heavy, unnecessarily
brought and unable to secure the result
expected, — would be like leaping into
deep water, unable to swim, and without
cause courting destruction and death."

"Shall we abandon Judaism?" When
you ask this question, you seem to forget
how many of us have virtually abandoned it in any sense that could be called
a religion. To how many has it become

little more than a form or a name, a
reminiscence, a sentiment and association, a custom which we cherish because
our fathers cherished it before us; a sort
of ancestor-worship which we accept or
reject because we are too lazy or too indifferent to examine for ourselves and
see whether religion could be anything
more or anything different, — so that it
ceases to be a matter of much consequence to ourselves, and still less to the
world at large, whether such a Judaism
be abandoned or not. It is true we have
not joined the dominant Church; but, as
we have seen, the ranks of the atheists,
and, above all, of agnosticism, have been
largely recruited from among us. On
the other hand, Judaism is too grand
and too sacred a heritage, and becomes
of too vital an import when it is a question of how we shall transmit it to our
children, to be allowed thus to go by de-

fault, to drift aimlessly into the shallows of indifferentism and unbelief, instead of deepening and broadening with the world's deeper spiritual currents, enriching and at the same time enriched thereby. Shall we be afraid of deep waters, — we, God's chosen ones, for whom the seas have divided, over whom again and again the waves and the billows have passed ? It is no sacrifice, no surrender we are called upon to make, but a coming to our own, a claiming of the kingdom which is ours for the taking, for the asking, for the seeking, where none is first, none last, but all are one in equal love and kinship, — a spiritual kingdom which is no far-away dream of the skies, no far-away dream of the earth, but here and now, in the heart and soul and mind of man ; the kingdom that is within us, every one of us who has the courage and faith to rise above our material surroundings and conditions, the world of time and space, beyond the things of sense, the things of earth, where heaven comes in sight. "As dying, and behold we live; as having nothing, and yet possessing all things."

But I must frankly confess that I have no ready-made creed, no ready-made church, no cut-and-dried formula of practice and belief to offer. The Christian Church, the Christian doctrine, holds no more for us than Judaism. The best Christianity of to-day is, for the most part, outside the churches and entirely outside of doctrine. Christianity is not, as we falsely suppose, a doctrine, — the doctrine of the Trinity, the Vicarious Sacrifice and Atonement, — although it is usually represented to us as such. Like Judaism, it is a life consecrated to God through loving service to man.

Where two or three are gathered together
in the name of this God who is Spirit, —
and who must be worshipped in spirit
and in truth, not in form, in the graven
image of the letter; not in outward service, but in the inner life of holiness and
peace, — shall we find our fellowship,
whether we be Jews or Gentiles. And
it is this fellowship that we must claim
if we would have any part in building
up the religion of the future, the "religion of humanity," as it is called. What
this religion may be, who can tell, who
can foresee? With what forms it may be
clothed, with what rites and symbols,
what of old truth or of new it may em-
body, we cannot know. But of one thing
we may be certain: there can be no true
religion, there can be no true humanity,
without this basis of fellowship. For the
rest we must be content to wait, to trust,
to hope, with so vast a hope before us,

so great a goal to be attained, so sure a light upon our path. And living thus in larger ideals, I cannot help believing that our lesser ills will fall away, our outer relations will adjust themselves in proportion as we come to a clearer understanding of ourselves. For each one of us the problem is an individual one, both as regards our outward circumstance and our inner convictions and experience; but according as we best solve it unto ourselves, so shall we best solve it unto others.

Rooted deep in our Judaism is a great moral force to sway the world, — the power which makes for righteousness, the Law which is like a seed buried in the dark earth. But the seed is not quickened except it die. Oh, for the quickening touch, the breath of the spirit that shall kindle with new life — God's life — this fiery seed, this immortal spark

of the soul, the knowledge of good and
evil, the hunger and thirst after righteousness! Like the strong and mighty wind
that sweeps over the earth, driving dead
things before it; like the sudden sunshine
that bursts the clouds and floods the air,
scattering radiance so that the depths are
kindled, the heights shine, the mighty sea
laughs and leaps like a child at play, and
each tiny bird-throat swells with its note
of praise and rapture, each tender flower-
bell rings out its fragrant carol for life,
dear life. The whole world is alive and
aflame with a light and glory not its own.
All creation is a pæan, a song of life triumphant, life universal, because " God
is in His heavens, God is in His world."

Ah, so shall the heart of man rejoice
when God has entered to fill and bless
it with His holy presence! " Eye hath
not seen, nor ear heard, neither have
entered into the heart of man, the things

which God hath prepared for them that
love Him." More tender than tenderest
flower of earth is the flower of heaven,—
love; more radiant than the sunlight,
mightier than the mighty wind or the
sea, is the great heart of man fashioned
in God's own image, to know and be
known of Him, gifted with God's great
gift of loving, the divine passion to know
and to do His will. As the tiny dewdrop
reflects the sun, so does the heart of man
reflect the great central sun, the glowing
soul of the universe, the life and light of
the world. Without this, all were dust
and ashes, crumbling before our eyes,
vanishing like an insubstantial dream;
our human lives were transient, perishable things, our joys a mockery, our
grief, despair. "The grass withereth,
the flower fadeth, but the word of God
(which is Love) endureth forever."
"Whether there be prophecies, they shall

fail: whether there be tongues, they shall cease: whether there be knowledge, it shall vanish away. Charity never faileth."

What we need is God in our hearts, in our life, — God with us in our midst, on our common earth, in our poor, distracted human lives. "For this mortal must put on immortality, this corruptible must put on incorruption." Not when we put on our grave-clothes and go down among the dead where none praise the Lord, but even now while we are still clothed in the flesh, wrapped round with human seeming and believing, must the spirit be free to burst its bonds and return unto God who gave it. When the veil of sense, the veil of self, is lifted, then is the heart made pure to see God; then only do we enter the spiritual life where the hidden things are revealed, the secret things of God made manifest, the deep, mysterious meanings of life unrolled. Sorrow and joy become as one in that beatific vision, and "heaven a daily reality of earth."

But think not that we inherit spiritual life because we are born into an inherited faith, an ancestral and traditional religion; because we preach a Unity or Trinity. Our life may be just as bare and unfruitful, our preaching just as unprofitable. God is not handed down to us in the sense that we hold Him in our hand firmly grasped and secure, ours only and theirs who believe as we do about Him, — in the sense that we have not to search for Him with all our heart and all our soul and all our mind, if haply we may find Him. On the contrary, He only comes to us out of a great heart-hunger and need, an infinite longing that will not be stilled, and that nothing else, nothing less, can satisfy or fill, — a deep experience of life, of human

joy and sorrow, that brings with it the
knowledge that because we have Him
not we die, and that in Him alone we
truly live. Such knowledge is life eternal, a knowing which is a being with
God that rests the soul and lifts it above
mortal conditions. For this came we
into the world, for this do we leave the
world in order that we may know eternal
life, — life ever more abundant; rest,
deep rest after weariness; joy beyond
pain, love stronger than death, — the
joy of which Jesus spoke when he had
drained the cup of sorrow to the dregs;
the peace that comes of perfect trust,
perfect faith, perfect oneness with the
Father. "Peace I leave with you, my
peace I give unto you; not as the world
giveth. . . . In the world ye shall have
tribulation; but be of good cheer, I have
overcome the world."

Teach us thus to know God, O teachers

of Israel who starve us on dry husks and formulas! It is for this we have been preserved; it is for this we are now scattered as the winds of heaven that nothing can hold or bind. Make us to drink of living waters, to love and be loved of Him who is the living God, —the God of the living and not of the dead, the loving Father of all. Take away the reproach of our people. "Wherefore should the heathen say, where is now their God? But our God is in the heavens; He hath done whatsoever He hath pleased." He hath bound and He can loose. Our God is in the earth, let all the world rejoice. "Let everything that hath breath praise the Lord." "So shall we not die but live, and declare the works of the Lord."

March, 1895.

EPILOGUE.

OF these essays, now for the first time collected and published in book form, the first appeared in the "Century Magazine" of January, 1892; the second, "The Outlook of Judaism," was written for the World's Parliament of Religions, and read before the Parliament in Chicago, September 16th, 1893. The others were published successively in the "Jewish Messenger," during the following eighteen months, and were, to some extent, answers to Jewish critics and exponents who dissented from my views. In offering them now to a larger public, I feel that an added word of explanation is necessary.

Hitherto I have addressed myself almost entirely to a Jewish public. It will be seen, I think, that I have told the truth *as I have seen it*, sparing and concealing nothing, making no apology, no justification, for my people, no appeal to any but themselves. For I have wished especially to lay stress upon the fact, that upon the Jews themselves rests the chief responsibility of their position, the throwing off of disabilities, the working out of their high destiny. Whatever the attitude of the Christians, however unjust, however unhuman, however un-Christian it may appear to us, all the more the Jew has it in his power to rise superior to it, to prove himself master and conqueror of his fate, when once he realises that redress lies within himself, that freedom and salvation are in his own hands.

But this is not to say that there is no other side to the question, no other help to its solution; that the Christians on their part have not a responsibility still more grave, — the responsibility of a wrong done instead of a wrong suffered, and therefore a duty still more plain, a redress still more urgent. Leroy Beaulieu says, " Hatred of the Jews is inspired not by Christian sentiment, but by anti-Christian instincts." In other words, anti-Semitism is anti-Christianity. Whoever takes it up is false to the very principles he would uphold, denies the very truth he would proclaim, and for the lack of which he persecutes the Jew. Not in the name of Judaism, but in the name of Christianity dishonoured and defaced, not the Jews therefore, but those who truly call themselves Christians, should protest against anti-Semitism. " There are in the world to-day seven or eight million Jews dispersed among four or five hundred million Christians or Moslems. We are apt to imagine," Leroy Beaulieu goes on to say, "that the great majority of the Jews of the world, or at least of Europe, are in possession of civil liberty and equality. This is a mistake. The Israelites who enjoy civic rights are still in a minority. The greater number of the descendants of Abraham are still subjected to restrictive laws. It may be true that this is mainly due to the fact that Russia alone contains more than half the Jews of the globe;" but it is also true that even in the most enlightened countries the Jew is under some sort of ban, whether moral or social, subject to some law of exception or exclusion, some disadvantage, some estrangement from his Christian neighbour.

Now, again, whatever the attitude of the Jews, whether or not their disabilities are inherent in themselves, I hold that this fact alone is a blot on Christianity, a failure on the part of a religion claiming to be the religion of equality and fraternity, and standing, as Christianity does to Judaism, in the relation of a religion to its parent religion, the religion which has given it birth, and to which the world owes so vast a debt as it does to Judaism. Dean Milman, the eminent historian of the Jews, says: " The religious obligations of mankind to the Jews it is impossible to appreciate in all their fulness." And another Christian authority, Professor D. G. Lyon, of Harvard University, in his address before the World's Parliament of Religions, in enumerating these obligations makes so striking a statement that he seems to cover almost the whole field of civilisation : " What has the Jew given us ?" he asks. " He has given us the Bible, the Old as well as the New Testament, which,

with the exception of one or possibly two
of its books, was written by men of Jewish
birth. . . . Along with the Sacred Writings have come to the race through the
Jews, certain great doctrines — Monotheism, — God's moral government of the
world, — His fatherhood, the brotherhood
of man, and the great types of humanity,
Abraham, Moses, Jeremiah, Paul. Jesus
himself was a Jew ; and Christianity then,
the religion which bears His name, is it
also a Jewish institution ? It has elements
which are not Jewish ; it has passed into
the keeping of those who are not Jews ;
but its earliest advocates and disciples, no
less than its founder, were Jews. The
first churches were Jewish. The chief
ordinances of the church, the service, the
prayers, still bear the stamp of their
Jewish origin ; and the Christian chari-
ties are but the embodiment of the Golden
Rule as uttered by a Jew. . . . Israel's

mission is peace, morality, and religion; or, better still, Israel's mission is peace through morality and religion. This, the nation's lesson to the world; this, the spirit of the greatest characters in Israel's history. To live in the same spirit; in a word, to become like the foremost of all Israelites, — this is the highest that any man has yet ventured to hope."

There is a saying of the Rabbis, " We men judge nations and classes too often only by the bad examples they produce; God judges them by their best and noblest types." If Israel be so judged then, it were to make him the type and pattern of humanity. But I do not ask this. I do not ask you thus to judge my people. Take us at our worst, as outcast and despised and rejected of men, — unto such above all comes the Christ, and so only can you prove your Christianity. " He that saith he is in the light and hateth his brother, is in darkness even until now." "He that loveth his brother abideth in the light, and there is none occasion of stumbling in him." Come to us not with fire and sword, with torture of the Inquisition, as you have come to us in the past; not with chapter and book and doctrine and text, as some are ready to come to us now, not with the letter, but the spirit — with love in your heart; love that redeems and transforms and transfigures, that takes away the sins of the world, blessing him that gives and him that takes; the love that is not in word, neither in tongue, but in deed and in truth. "For hereby do we know that ye are of the truth."

1. "Day long I brooded upon the Passion of Israel.

2. I saw him bound to the wheel,

nailed to the cross, cut off by the sword, burned at the stake, tossed into the seas.

3. And always the patient, resolute martyr face arose in silent rebuke and defiance.

4. A Prophet with four eyes; wide-gazed the orbs of the spirit above the sleeping eyelids of the senses.

5. A Poet, who plucked from his bosom the quivering heart and fashioned it into a lyre.

6. A placid-browed Sage, uplifted from earth in celestial meditation.

7. These I saw, with princes and people in their train; the monumental dead, and the standard-bearers of the future.

8. And suddenly I heard a burst of mocking laughter; and turning, I beheld the shuffling gait, the ignominious features, the sordid mask of the son of the Ghetto."

Turn again, O daughter of Israel, my sister, and behold with divinely awakened eyes the son of man, the man of sorrows and acquainted with grief. " Inasmuch as ye have done it unto one of the least of these my brethren, ye have done it unto me." Who has ever spoken words so tender and close, so fulfilled of the brotherhood of man ? " And I, if I be lifted, will draw all men up unto me."

Be ye then uplifted, ye who would uplift. Ye who come in his name and yet deny him, with Christ on your lips but with hatred and scorn in your heart, behold the suffering child of God, your brother ; behold our divine humanity crushed beneath the burden of the flesh, the sins and sorrows of the world ! Ye who would bear witness to his spirit and his truth, to the Christ that is within you, look with the eyes of Christ, the heart of Christ ; pierce with illumined vision the hollow mask ; let the warm rays, the gentle touch of love, fall upon the dull clod of clay, and awake the sleeping soul, the higher, the divine self that slumbers in every child of earth, every one of God's creatures, — the Christ that is to be, when all men know themselves as he knew, one with the Father and one with his fellow-man.

March, 1895.

THE END.